I0815874

Yoga of the Natural State

Yoga of the Natural State

The Dzogchen Aural Lineage

Longchen Rabjam

TRANSLATED BY
Ācārya Malcolm Smith

Edited by Osa Karen Manell

Wisdom Publications
with Zangthal Editions

Wisdom Publications
132 Perry Street
New York, NY 10014 USA
wisdom.org

Library of Congress Cataloging-in-Publication Data
Names: Klong-chen-pa Dri-med-'od-zer, 1308–1363 author |
Smith, Malcolm (Buddhism practitioner) translator
Title: Yoga of the natural state: the Dzogchen aural lineage /
Longchen Rabjam; translated by Ācārya Malcolm Smith.
Description: New York, NY, USA: Wisdom, [2025] |
Includes bibliographical references and index.
Identifiers: LCCN 2025009554 (print) | LCCN 2025009555 (ebook) |
ISBN 9781614299622 hardcover | ISBN 9781614299820 ebook
Subjects: LCSH: Klong-chen-pa Dri-med-'od-zer, 1308-1363 |
Rnying-ma-pa (Sect)—Doctrines | Rdzogs-chen
Classification: LCC BQ7950.K667 S6513 2025 (print) |
LCC BQ7950.K667 (ebook) | DDC 294.3/923—dc23/eng/20250909
LC record available at https://lccn.loc.gov/2025009554
LC ebook record available at https://lccn.loc.gov/2025009555

ISBN 978-1-61429-962-2 ebook ISBN 978-1-61429-982-0

29 28 27 26 25 5 4 3 2 1

Cover design by Marc Whitaker. Interior design by Gopa & Ted2.
Typeset by PerfecType.

Printed on acid-free paper that meets the guidelines for permanence and durability of the Production Guidelines for Book Longevity of the Council on Library Resources.

Printed in Canada.

Contents

Dedication

This book is dedicated to the memory of Rigzin Kunzang Dechen Lingpa.

Translator's Introduction

Thus I heard it said at one time. The teaching of the Buddha began as an aural lineage. It is unclear from the archaeological record whether writing existed in India at the time of the Buddha, and there are conflicting opinions. It is commonly agreed that the first texts containing the Buddha's teachings were committed to writing during the first century before the common era, and this appears to be true for both what are commonly referred to as the "mainstream" traditions, such as Sthaviravāda, and so on, and the burgeoning Mahāyāna movement. In almost every case, these written texts, called *sūtras*, purporting to contain the actual words of the Buddha, begin with the phrase "Thus I heard it said at one time." All later Buddhist sūtras as well as the tantras present themselves as the Buddha's speech (Skt. *vacana*, Tib. *bka'*), either directly, by permission, or through blessings. Thus, the path of a practitioner who wishes to engage in the trio of wisdoms—hearing, reflection, and contemplation—begins with hearing a Buddhist teacher. Hearing, rather than reading, is how a journey begins into the heart of the wisdom taught by the Buddha.

We can understand that all Buddhist teachings are based on aural lineages, whether we consider the transmission of the early Buddhist sūtras or formal study in monastic universities in India, China, Tibet, Japan, and so on. Tibet, in particular, traditionally confers important texts through the reading transmission, considered indispensable and without which one does not possess the complete transmission of a text, the body of knowledge it represents, or its blessings.

While the textual lineage (*dpe brgyud*) of the Great Perfection tradition is widely known, little attention has been paid to its aural lineages (*nyan brgyud, rna brgyud*). *Yoga of the Natural State* is a presentation, for the first time in English, of the most important aural lineage associated with the Great Perfection. It includes a series of texts first written in the mid-fourteenth century by Longchenpa (1308–64). The introduction below locates this aural lineage within the larger spectrum of aural lineages associated with the Great Perfection tradition and identifies specific features distinguishing this aural lineage from the others.

The Historical Context of the Great Perfection

The Indian antecedents for what has become known in Tibet as *rdzogs pa chen po*, the Great Perfection, grew out of a trenchant skepticism toward the liberative effectiveness of the ritualized Buddhist practice we now call Vajrayāna, as well as skepticism toward the grand vision of liberation over three incalculable eons that we find in mainstream Indian Mahāyāna. This skepticism has been carried forward by Tibetan adherents of the Great Perfection tradition to the present day, even while many of them are also fully engaged in Vajrayāna ritualism.

The fundamental argument of the Great Perfection in all its expressions is that awakening is not the result of cause and effect and cannot be achieved through effort. The Great Perfection takes quite literally the Buddha's description of awakening found in the *Lalitavistara Sūtra* that buddhahood is peaceful, uncompounded, pure, free from all proliferation, and blissful. Accordingly, awakening is something to be discovered in the direct perception of *dharmatā* rather than generated through causes.

Between the introduction of the Great Perfection to Tibet in the last quarter of the eighth century and the second influx of Buddhism from India during the latter part of the tenth century and the eleventh century, the communities in which the Great Perfection teachings spread were very active, given the evidence of the large number of texts on the Great Perfection that can be dated before 1200 CE. Following this, during the period of Buddhist institutional reconsolidation, which began during the eleventh century, Tibetans would choose whether they continued with the indigenous expressions of the Dharma that grew out of the early diffusion of Buddhism in the eighth and ninth centuries

(Nyingma and Bön) or abandon these for newer forms of Vajrayāna imported to Tibet, such as those flourishing in the Indian monastic universities of Vikramaśilā, Nālandā, Somapura, and elsewhere, such as the Buddhist communities in the Kathmandu Valley and Kashmir. A prime example of this is Khön Könchok Gyalpo's (1034–1102) tentative abandonment of the Khön clan's hereditary teachings in favor of the Hevajra and Cakrasaṃvara teachings newly imported to Tibet. The eleventh century also witnessed the rise of the Bön tradition as a viable tradition, even if politically and socially isolated, whose principal Great Perfection teaching is the *Aural Lineage of Zhang Zhung*.

The evidence suggests that Tibetan Great Perfection adherents did not passively wait out the chaos brought about by the collapse of the Tang dynasty and unrest in Central Asia due to Arab military adventures in the region. This is quite clear, given that Great Perfection texts, tantric rituals, and Chan literature were found side by side on the outskirts of the Tibetan empire in the Dunhuang caves, which were closed in the early eleventh century. In various places in Tibet and Kham, tantric lineages such as Vajrakilāya were actively practiced, and Tibetan adepts such as Vairocana, Yudra Nyingpo, Nubchen Sangyé Yeshé, Aro Yeshé Jungné, and so on, were active in promulgating the teachings of the Great Perfection as a tradition divorced from and superior to the ritualized forms of tantric Buddhism brought to Tibet with royal support during the imperial period. The Great Perfection literature we have received clearly reflects the indigenous interests and needs of a community of Tibetan scholars and practitioners whose time is obscure to us and to Tibetan historians due to internal and external military, political, and social upheaval in and around Tibet between 840 CE and 970 CE.

The Great Perfection's own narratives across all genres consistently report that the Great Perfection teachings were regarded with trepidation and fear by Tibetan religious and secular elites. The background for this anxiety is the famed Samyé debate between the Indian *paṇḍita* Kamalaśīla and the Chinese *bhikṣu* Hashang Mahāyāna, which led to the Tibetan elite's adoption of the gradualist position of Indian Buddhism as the state-sanctioned form of Buddhism in toto. Consequently, the Great Perfection was promulgated within a limited circle of practitioners who were not afraid to explore the buddhahood that was free from a cause and who had the religious maturity not to use it as an excuse for blatant antinomian conduct.

To contextualize the Great Perfection with the Nyingma school, the latter defines six grades of tantras: a class of three outer tantras—*kriyā*, *ubhaya*, and yoga—which lacks a completion stage and mainly focuses on ritual, and a class of three inner tantras—mahāyoga, anuyoga, and atiyoga—which mainly focuses on *samādhi*. The Nyingma school places tantras such as the *Guhyasamāja*, *Guhyagarbha*, and so on, within the category of mahāyoga, which places great emphasis on a gradual process of creation, the imagined construction of a celestial mansion and its deities.

In particular, the *Guhyagarbha* is considered the basic tantra of the Nyingma school because its thirteenth chapter describes the state of the Great Perfection. Based on this fact and other sources, some Western historians conclude that the Great Perfection did not originally exist as an independent tradition and attempt to locate its origin in this source text, framing the Great Perfection principally as a development of the early reception of the mahāyoga class of tantras. However, they will readily admit this assessment does not find support within the earliest extant commentaries of the tradition of the Great Perfection itself. This view, common among Western historians, is in stark contrast with the traditional Nyingma view, which characterizes the Great Perfection as an independent tradition from the start, with its own texts, lineages, and traditions.

Some of this confusion stems from the fact that the Great Perfection tradition can and does utilize the appearance of Vajrayāna ritualism in conferring empowerments. However, unlike the traditions of mahāyoga and anuyoga, the Great Perfection does not depend on such rituals for its transmission. Instead, the Great Perfection depends on an indispensable transmission of a type of empowerment called "the potentiality of *vidyā* empowerment" (*rig pa'i rtsal dbang*), during which the student is introduced to the state of the great perfection through words, symbols, and ultimately through joining the teacher in the same state of knowledge (*vidyā*). This knowledge is not an ordinary kind of knowledge;

rather, it is knowledge of the pristine consciousness that forms the basis for one's continuum.

Another difference between the Great Perfection and other systems generally classified under the rubric of Vajrayāna is that its underlying theory connected with the basis of purification, purifier, and the result of purification is completely different from that found in the standardized system of four empowerments derived from the later Indian tradition. In general, the basis of purification in mahāyoga is the impure five aggregates, twelve sense bases, and eighteen sense elements. The purifier of the basis of purification is the sequence of visualizations of the maṇḍala that the practitioner runs through systematically. The result of purification is the actualization of the transformation of the impure basis, the sentient being, into a fully awakened buddha. Since the view of the Great Perfection is that all phenomena of the aggregates, sense bases, and sense elements are intrinsically pure from the beginning, the basis of purification is the ignorance (Skt. *avidyā*, Tib. *ma rig pa*) that does not recognize this fact. The purifier is direct introduction into this knowledge (Skt. *vidyā*, Tib. *rig pa*) by a qualified guru and practicing that knowledge as the path. The result of purification is recognizing one's innate state of buddhahood.

Lastly, there is a difference regarding deity practices. While Great Perfection cycles do have Vajrayāna deity practices connected with them, those typically exist as ancillary practices for longevity, removing obstacles, and other secondary considerations supportive of the practice of the Great Perfection itself. Thus, the Great Perfection cannot be reduced to merely a branch of Vajrayāna ritualism, especially because of the trenchant critiques the core texts of the Great Perfection make of Vajrayāna methods and goals.

Nor can we reduce the Great Perfection to merely being the culmination of the process of the creation stage and the completion stage. The creation stage amounts to generating and identifying with a complex maṇḍala or even a simple form of a deity such as Avalokiteśvara. The completion stage focuses on dissolving that maṇḍala or deity into the empty mind essence to eliminate self-grasping and includes practices like so-called "inner heat yoga," various kinds of *prāṇāyāma*, and even erotic practices. Jamgön Kongtrul, the nineteenth-century doyen of the nonsectarian movement, noted that the Great Perfection cannot be considered a mere add-on to the process of these two stages:

> Here, the basis of the stage (*rim*) of the meditation of atiyoga, the pinnacle of the nine *yānas*, is not the culmination of creation (*bskyed*), completion (*rdzogs*), and great completion (*rdzogs pa chen po*). When inferred from the term, *mahāsandhi* [*rdzogs pa chen po*] should be translated as *mahāsamādhi* or *mahādhyāna*, meaning that all phenomena of saṃsāra and nirvāṇa are unsurpassed, self-arisen pristine consciousness within the dimension of the sole reality, which transcends the intellectual *siddhāntas* of the eight lower *yānas*.[1]

Thus, the insistence of some in asserting that the Great Perfection must be grounded in the mahāyoga tantras translated during the earlier diffusion of Buddhism into Tibet serves only to erase the indigenous voice of this tradition as a whole. When Great Perfection exponents identify the Great Perfection as an independent tradition apart from the ritual traditions of the yoga and mahāyoga tantras, it should be taken seriously.

Moreover, Western academic interest has focused primarily on divining the philosophical underpinnings of the Great Perfection tradition, without acknowledging that the Great Perfection tradition itself eschews the kind of intellectual analysis Western attention is focused upon. Over and over again, practitioners and authors of the Great Perfection tradition tell us that the Great Perfection is not a philosophy and that the meaning of the Great Perfection cannot be reached through exercises in intellectual analysis. The eleventh-century master Rongzom Chökyi Zangpo tells us in his *Introduction to Mahāyāna Systems* that while the Great Perfection cannot be proven through syllogistic reasoning, neither can it be negated through that same reasoning, summoning the arguments raised against epistemological argumentation

1. Jamgön Kongtrul, *Catalogue of the Treasury of Precious Instructions*, p. 422.

by Nāgārjuna. However, the Great Perfection tradition is not anti-intellectual, and its primary and secondary literature devotes some attention to pointing out the deficits of other traditions, non-Buddhist and Buddhist. The purpose of these critiques is to eliminate unwarranted conceptual proliferation, following the tradition of Buddhist *siddhānta* literature in general.

The primary distinction that the Great Perfection draws between itself and the Buddhism of the *yānas* is based on the difference between inference and direct perception. The Great Perfection tradition holds that the approach of the Buddhism of the yānas is inferential and analytical, and thus intellectual and conceptual. Since the Great Perfection itself is based on direct perception, it is nonanalytical—thus beyond the intellect—and therefore nonconceptual.

The Great Perfection tradition does not oppose sūtra or Vajrayāna practices. It shares the same existential goal as all Buddhist traditions: ending rebirth caused by affliction and karma. Rather, it opposes the idea that the meaning of the Buddha's awakening can be reached by relying upon effort and perceiving awakening as a result born of a cause. Nevertheless, in the *Cultivation of Bodhicitta* composed by Mañjuśrīmitra, one of the five Great Perfection texts brought to Tibet by Vairocana during the late eighth century, there is a reference to an indirect approach for discovering the meaning of the Great Perfection. Great Perfection adepts understood that not everyone can directly enter the knowledge of the state of great perfection beyond cause and result and thus some need a more gradual approach.

The interest in resorting to apotropaic and erotic rites found in cycles connected with Vajrakilāya, Guhyagarbha, and so on, does not contradict a lack of confidence in the effectiveness of the cause-and-result approach to Buddhist liberation. As Rongzom notes in the *Introduction to Mahāyāna Systems*:

> The path sought with methods involving effort should be taught to those who are unable to abide in the approach of the Great Perfection just as they are. However, that path should also be connected with the view of the Great Perfection. Why?

> Because the great bliss of bodhicitta is the root of the Dharma
> able to expel all illness of bondage.[2]

Although a nod is given here to people of lower caliber based upon their inability to readily discern the state of the Great Perfection, the cause-and-result approach of the eight or nine yānas is regarded as merely palliative and ultimately must be seen to be false and abandoned. The subitist rhetoric of the Great Perfection, widely regarded as subversive, panicked Tibetan elites both during the imperial period, leading to the exile of Vairocana, and later at the beginning of the second influx of Indian Buddhism into Tibet. It remains a cause of institutional anxiety to the present day, with the widespread exportation of Vajrayāna to the West.

It should be observed that skepticism about the necessity of practicing the two stages was also quite evident in India as well as Tibet, even in the eighth and ninth centuries. A group of such skeptics—Śrī Siṃha,[3] Padmasambhava's guru Bhikṣuṇī Nandi, and the Blue-Skirted Paṇḍita,[4] a favorite villain of Tibetan historians—is singled out in a text by the mid-tenth-century Indian scholar Mañjuśrīkīrti[5] as an Indian movement that considered the creation stage unnecessary at best. This skepticism is also evident throughout the *dohā*s of mahāsiddhas such as Saraha, Tilopa, and Virūpa and in the circle of Maitrīpa and his students.[6]

In addition to the charge of subitist heresy, we can much better understand the polemical reaction to the Great Perfection during the imperial period and from the eleventh century onward if we begin with Lha

2. Rongzom Chökyi Zangpo, *Introduction to Mahāyāna Systems*, p. 133b.

3. A *Rnam par snang mdzad* is also singled out. Perhaps this list was compiled based on a Tibetan informant.

4. This character is often singled out in Tibetan historical sources as someone who introduced Tibetans to incorrect tantric practices of union and liberation. Jigten Sumgön, the renowned founder of Drikung, accuses the Blue-Skirted Paṇḍita of mixing Buddhist teachings with Bönpo teachings and hiding them as treasures.

5. Mañjuśrīkīrti, *Ornament of the Heart*, p. 238b.

6. See Mathes, *Maitrīpa: India's Yogi of Nondual Bliss* (Boulder: Shambhala Publications, 2001), pp. 124–26.

Lama Yeshé Wo's decree, *Refutation of False Mantra* (*Sngags log sun byin*). These later polemics systematically targeted the Great Perfection as an indigenous movement lacking satisfactory sources in Indian Buddhist traditions, criticizing it alongside the deviations attributed to the Blue-Skirted Paṇḍita, Ācārya Marpo, and other villains of Tibetan history.

The influential eleventh-century translator Gö Khugpa Lhetse claims in his *Refutation of False Mantra* that Vairocana forged the five early mind series texts, stating that when the forgery was discovered, Vairocana was exiled by the king and ministers to the kingdom of Gyalrong in east Tibet. Gö accuses Nub Sangyé Yeshé[7] of composing many false teachings and similarly targets Aro Yeshé Jungné. The thirteenth-century translator Chag Lotsawa echoes these complaints, claiming that Vairocana composed the five early mind series texts motivated by pride, asserting in general that these early adepts were conflating non-Buddhist and Bönpo tenets with Buddhist tenets, thereby creating false doctrines. Chag Lotsawa also targets the Chö of Machik Labdrön,[8] illustrating that from the eleventh through the thirteenth centuries, elite Buddhist scholars also held newer indigenous forms of tantric Buddhism, as well as the Great Perfection, in extremely low regard. These polemics stifled the open dissemination of the Great Perfection movement, especially from the eleventh to the fourteenth centuries, and forced its adherents underground, who then pretended to observe the norms promulgated by Tibetan exponents of newfangled Indian Vajrayāna.

As the mainstream Buddhist institutions in Tibet forged ahead receiving and formulating the Buddhism of the day as it was found by them in the monasteries and universities of India that flourished during the Pāla dynasty, some tenth-, eleventh-, and twelfth-century

7. *Nubs Sangs rgyas Ye shes* (832–942) was the first Tibetan to write a systematic presentation comparing Indian gradualism, Chinese subitism, mahāyoga tantra, and the Great Perfection traditions, the *Lamp for the Eye of Concentration* (*Bsam gtan mig sgron*). The *Lamp for the Eye of Concentration* was lost for centuries until its republication in 1974. Among its features, it portrays Chinese subitism as superior to Indic gradualism, in stark contrast to the official position of most Tibetan schools.

8. *Ma gcig Lab sgron* (1055–1149), renowned for founding the system of Chö, or Severance. Her system of practice based in the Perfection of Wisdom has spread within all schools of Tibetan Buddhism.

Great Perfection adherents responded with their own polemics. These rebuttals were largely ignored, and the works of these authors barely survived, quickly subsiding into obscurity. Religious movements generally only rise to prominence with the support of the elite, the Great Perfection being no exception to this rule. The Great Perfection only began to regain respectability during the fourteenth century due to the patronage of important and wealthy religious figures such as the Third Karmapa Rangjung Dorjé, Tai Situ Changchub Gyaltsen, and others.

An unfortunate side effect of the derogation of the Great Perfection tradition from the eleventh to the fourteenth centuries was the loss of so much of its early literature. However, despite the general institutional hostility observable in the Kadampa, Sakya, and even Kagyü traditions toward the Great Perfection in the eleventh, twelfth, and thirteenth centuries, the Great Perfection tradition was preserved through the promulgation of several subaltern strands of aural lineage traditions isolated from and largely invisible to the main centers of institutional Buddhism. Despite the efforts of the so-called "nonsectarian movement" in modern times, hostility, indifference, and skepticism toward the Great Perfection has hardly abated among the larger Tibetan Buddhist institutions, apart from the Nyingma and Bön traditions, and its own narratives have met with skepticism.

Overview of the Great Perfection Aural Lineages

Before we begin to examine the aural lineage preserved by Longchenpa, it is important to provide an overview of the range of Great Perfection aural lineages. Since the twelfth century, Great Perfection lineages and literature have been divided into three main categories: the mind series (*sems sde*), the space series (*klong sde*), and the intimate instruction series (*man ngag sde*). This scheme is found in the commentarial literature of the so-called *cittatilaka* (*snying thig*) or "core potential" class of Great Perfection teachings, beginning with the *Great Chronicle* composed by Tashi Dorjé. These three series include all the Great Perfection teachings introduced to Tibet by the students of Śṛi Siṃha (ca. eighth century CE), the Indian scholar Vimalamitra (?–810 CE), and the Tibetan translator Vairocana (ca. 750–850 CE).

These three Great Perfection lineages can be subdivided into two: the aural lineages and the textual or explanatory lineages (*dpe/bshad brgyud*). Generally, an aural lineage is a lineage passed down from a realized teacher to a student, one-to-one. The *Treasury of Siddhānta*[9] states:

> The essence of the aural lineage is the close connection of an actual one-to-one lineage. The nature of the aural lineage is being uninterrupted, because it is related to those of sharp faculties. The characteristic of the aural lineage is trustworthiness, because it is free from error. When divided, the written and unwritten aural lineages occur as intimate instructions of words and meanings.
>
> The essence of the explanatory lineage is the absence of returning to the three realms, because there is no cause to do so in the dharmatā devoid of effort, self-originated pristine consciousness. The nature of the explanatory lineage is the recognition of the five pristine consciousnesses, because luminosity is stainless. The characteristic of the explanatory lineage is the transcendent state of the three *kāya*s and the five pristine consciousnesses abiding permanently, because that transcendent state transcends intellectual analysis.[10]

While some treasure revelations (*gter ma*) are referred to as aural lineages—for example, the core texts of the *Dgongs pa zang thal* revelations of Rigzin Godem—here the discussion will be confined to the so-called *bka' ma* or "spoken" teachings. The textual lineage is the support for the aural lineage, and the aural lineage supports the textual lineage. Thus, while the main Western academic focus has been on Great

9. *Siddhānta*, or *grub mtha'*, often translated as "tenet" or "philosophical conclusion," literally means "established conclusion." I have opted to preserve the Sanskrit term, as the term *grub mtha'* is also used for the realization of the goal of a specific meditation system.

10. Drimé Özer (Longchenpa), *Treasury of Siddhānta*, pp. 1165–66.

Perfection explanatory lineages, the core of the Great Perfection is in fact to be found in the extant records we have of the Great Perfection aural lineages. The indigenous perspective on the relative importance of textual versus aural transmission is shown by the great reverence held for the Great Perfection aural lineages set down by Khenpo Ngawang Palzang in the *Command Sealed* (*bka' rgya ma*) volume of his collected works. These texts represent the experiential teachings of masters associated with the renowned treasure cycle, the *Longchen Nyingtik*. These transmissions are significantly more important than the less restricted Dzogchen material belonging to the same cycle and much more difficult to receive, even though their content is doctrinally not substantially different from Jigmé Lingpa's manual, *Unsurpassed Pristine Consciousness* (*Ye shes bla ma*).

The Aural Lineages of the Mind Series

The mind series comprises a group of twenty-one core texts that generally have the term *bodhicitta* (*byang chub sems*) or "pure, perfect mind" in their title. The most well-known is the *All-Creating King* (*Kun byed rgyal po*). These twenty-one texts are foundational for the Great Perfection tradition as a whole, and many commentaries on these texts have been recovered from obscurity thanks to the publication efforts of the late Khenpo Munsel (1916–94).

The aural lineage texts of the mind series, as distinct from the mind series texts themselves, are included in three texts and one collection: Dorjé Pal's *Empowerment Rite of the Mind Series*, which presents in empowerment format the eighteen vajra songs of the masters of the mind series lineage coming through Vairocana's disciple, Yudra Nyingpo (ninth century), and found in Vairocana's biography;[11] Namkha Dorjé's *Detailed Manual of the Mind Series*, which details the Kham tradition; and Khachö Wangpo's *Easy Manual of the Center of the Sky*,

11. See Ani Jinba Palmo, *The Great Image* (Boulder: Shambhala Publications, 2004).

which summarizes the Aro tradition. Finally, the expanded Nyingma Kama[12] has a large collection of instructions from the Aro tradition.

As mentioned above, the empowerment of the potential of vidyā (*rig pa'i rtsal dbang*) is the primary means of transmitting the Great Perfection teachings. The *Precious Lamp*, the commentary for the *Realms and Transformations of Sound Tantra*, specifies that it is important to receive the eighteen empowerments of the potential of vidyā connected to the mind series as a prerequisite for receiving the empowerments for the cittatilaka teachings, setting out the mind series as the fundamental basis for all Great Perfection teachings. These eighteen empowerments, found in Dorjé Pal's *Empowerment Rite of the Mind Series*, are based on the vajra songs of eighteen of the so-called twenty-one "learned ones" (*mkhas pa*),[13] beginning with King Dahenatalo. These vajra songs concern the essential meaning of each of the eighteen mind series *lungs*,[14] which are further summarized in eighteen aural lineages, single-line statements summarizing the essence of the *lung* with which they are connected. While part of the Nyang tradition, this transmission is considered the universal system for giving empowerment into the mind series system itself. The practice instructions for the Nyang system are found in Lödro Gyaltsen's *Manual of the Great Perfection Mind Series*.

Next is Namkha Dorjé's *Detailed Manual of the Mind Series*, which details the Kham tradition. This practice manual emphasizes a gradual approach to Dzogchen teachings through the practice of the four samādhis: the state of calm (*gnas pa*), the state of imperturbability (*mi g.yo ba*), the state of uniformity (*mnyam nyid*), and the state of effortlessness (*lhun grub*). In reality, the four samādhis are not the result of one-pointed concentration; rather, they are stages in the gradual process of discovering one's own primordial basis (*ye gzhi*).

Khachö Wangpo's *Easy Manual of the Center of the Sky* summarizes

12. *Bka' ma* is a Nyingma term used to distinguish long lineage traditions, in contrast to the short lineage of the treasure tradition.

13. These twenty-one adepts are not a sequential lineage; rather, they are in groups of seven from three generations.

14. In this context the term *lung*, a translation of the Sanskrit term *āgama*, refers to an extract of a larger text.

the preliminaries of the Aro tradition. A second text called the *Detailed Manual of the Essence of Bodhicitta: The Precious Aural Lineage* is included as an appendix and precisely details the view, meditation, conduct, and result of Dzogchen. In addition, a collection of the thirty-eight instructions of the Aro aural lineage was edited from a manuscript said to belong to Jowo Yeshé, a disciple of the twelfth-century adept Zhikpo Dütsi.[15] Both the Kham lineage and the Aro lineage pass through Zhikpo Dütsi.

The Aural Lineages of the Space Series

Next, we turn our attention to the aural lineages of the space series, the *Vajra Bridge Aural Lineage*.[16] This cycle is based on a short root text composed by Vairocana and forms the foundation for the practice of the space series. This is supplemented by three commentaries composed by the twelfth-century author Kunzang Dorjé: the long, middle-length, and short explanations. In addition, there are accompanying empowerments, *sādhanas*, and various ancillary texts found in the main section of the Kama. A related set of space series texts was also edited by Yeshé Jungden (dates unknown), which probably date to the eleventh century.[17] This series of twenty-one texts is attributed to various authors such as Garab Dorjé, Bhikṣuṇī Nandi, Kukuripa, and so on, concluding with a commentary by Yeshé Jungden.

There is no evidence of any of the twelfth-century Vajra Bridge texts displaying knowledge of the intimate instruction series literature. Although the term "three series" is used, its use is completely different than the familiar mind, space, and intimate instruction series:

> The position of general dharma is the dharma taught by three teachers. In that regard, the dharmas taught by the *dharmakāya*

15. See Zhikpo Dütsi, *Aural Lineage of Aro Yeshé Jungney*.

16. *Bka' ma shin tu rgyas pa*, vol. 32, pp. 7–476.

17. For example, Kunzang Dorjé's *Long Explanation*, p. 233, cites the *Precious Light*, an aural lineage text from Śrī Siṃha found in Yeshé Jungden's collection.

> teacher Śrī Samantabhadra are three: the restorative series (*'chos sde*), the tantra series (*rgyud sde*), and the space series (*klong sde*). For whom are those intended? [Those are intended] for the continuums of all sentient beings. Since they abide in the delusion of misunderstanding because of ignorance, the mahāyoga creation stage is taught as the restorative series for people of the average of the highest caliber to restore them into nondelusion. The *āgamas* (*lung*) of anuyoga are taught as the tantra series to people of the medium of the highest caliber to show that the meaning of *nondelusion* is "uninterrupted." Great Perfection atiyoga is taught as the space series to people of the highest of the highest caliber to show that the meaning of *uninterrupted* is "inexhaustible" and "unchanging."[18]

The text goes on to explain that the saṃbhogakāya teacher is Vairocana, who teaches the three lower tantras to those of middling caliber, and the nirmāṇakāya teacher is Śākyamuni, who teaches the three causal vehicles to those of average caliber. Here, *kriya, upa*, and *yoga* are defined as the outer three series (*phyi pa sde gsum*) of secret mantra. Also, *vinaya, abhidharma*, and *sūtra* are the three series taught by Śākyamuni.

In Kunzang Dorjé's works, the term *vajra bridge* is defined in this way: "Since the transcendent state of the buddhas is the uninterrupted stream of the vajra of ultimate dharmatā, it is called the *vajra bridge*." We should understand that the term *vajra bridge* is widespread. For example, in the *Unwritten Aural Lineage of Cutting Saṃsāra from the Root*, Śrī Siṃha states:

> This aural lineage of the vajra bridge
> descending from the teacher of the three kāyas
> is the domain of those of highest caliber.
> How sad it is for misfortunate, confused ones!

However, a later interpretation by Chökyi Drakpa holds the term *vajra*

18. Kunzang Dorjé, *Middle-Length Explanation*, pp. 345–46.

bridge to mean that the space series is a bridge that serves to connect the mind series with the intimate instruction series:

> In the trio of the mind series, space series, and intimate instruction series, mahāmudrā, pacification, severance, and so on, are equivalent with the mind series. The aural lineage of the Vajra Bridge is the space series, which also is defined in three series. As for *vajra bridge*, *vajra* is a special word of mantra. An *ācārya* is a vajra ācārya, a disciple is a vajra disciple, a Dharma is called a vajra word, and so on. *Bridge* means that the mind series and the intimate instruction series are connected by the space series; thus it is a bridge. As it connects two bodies—able to transform the body of this life into a rainbow body—[the space series] can also be called a bridge.[19]

Thus, the Vajra Bridge tradition is also an important aural lineage in the Great Perfection tradition. It too has garnered little attention from Western historians, and in modern times only my teacher, the late Chögyal Namkhai Norbu (1938–2018), has revived this as a living practice tradition.

The Aural Lineage of the Intimate Instruction Series

This aural lineage is preserved in the curricular writings of the fourteenth-century author commonly known as Longchenpa. Specifically, this aural lineage is preserved in his *Lama Yangtik* (*Bla ma yang tig*) and *Zabmo Yangtik* (*Zab mo yang tig*) collections.

There are four reasons why these texts are worthy of our attention. First, the overall structure of Longchenpa's aural lineage writings is defined by the system of the six *bardo*s and the six lamps. These two schemes are widely used in later Great Perfection literature but do not seem to have been in common use before the fourteenth century. Second, while many of Longchenpa's writings are difficult to understand,

19. *Opening the Eyes of the Fortunate*, pp. 425–26.

with daunting terminology, by contrast his aural lineage writings are easy to understand, straightforward, written in relatively simple language rich with similes and metaphors, and easy to practice. Third, as this system of instruction has been until now overlooked in the West, it is important to present these teachings in English to those people who are interested in the practice of the Great Perfection. Fourth, these teachings have been passed down mouth-to-ear from the time of Garab Dorjé until the present day and are crucial for preserving the Great Perfection for the benefit of sentient beings in the future, for reasons we will understand later.

All evidence suggests that the *Lama Yangtik* was written first, shortly after Longchenpa completed a long retreat after leaving his guru Kumarāja, and that the *Zabmo Yangtik* was written sometime later. The chronological difficulty with Longchenpa's writings is that he generally did not date them, and we only have a rough idea of the order of their composition. However, we can say with certainty that he wrote about the aural lineage in the *Lama Yangtik* first and continued to elucidate it in the second volume of the *Zabmo Yangtik*, which concludes with the lengthy supporting commentary, the *Profound Mirror*.

Longchenpa was an inveterate composer of chronicles for the Great Perfection, because chronicles (*lo rgyus*) play an important role in the tradition. The *Union of the Sun and Moon Tantra* states:

> If the topic of the chronicle is not explained,
> there will be the fault of a lack of confidence
> in this oral lineage of the definitive great secret.

Longchenpa composed one chronicle of the Great Perfection lineage for the *Lama Yangtik* and two chronicles for the *Zabmo Yangtik*: one chronicle for the standard cittatilaka lineage and one chronicle for the aural lineage. Longchenpa bases all these chronicles on the *Great Chronicle* composed by Tashi Dorjé. The most extensive one appears in the *Profound Mirror* from the *Zabmo Yangtik*. In addition, he composed a chronicle for the *Khandro Nyingtik* cycle.

The lineage of the aural lineage is the same as the cittatilaka lineage: Garab Dorjé, Mañjuśrīmitra, Śrī Siṃha, Jñānasūtra, Vimalamitra, and so on, up to Chetsun Sengé Wangchuk. According to the *Lama Yangtik*'s *Precious Garland Chronicle*, after being written down by Garab Dorjé, the arrangement of the Great Perfection tantras was left to Mañjuśrīmitra, who divided them into three series. In particular, he divided the intimate instruction teachings into an aural lineage and an explanatory lineage (also termed the "textual lineage"). The *Precious Garland Chronicle* notes:

> Then, Ācārya Mañjuśrīmitra divided the Dharma of the Natural Great Perfection into the trio of the mind series, space series, and intimate instruction series. Next, having divided the dharma of the supreme cittatilaka included among those three series into an aural lineage and an explanatory lineage, he set down the secret aural lineages in notes for those of gradual caliber. Unable to find a suitable recipient for the explanatory lineage, he concealed the texts as a treasure beneath a boulder with a crossed vajra to the northeast of Vajrāsana.[20]

There are two points of interest here: the first is that the aural lineage of the cittatilaka teachings is set down in notes; the second is that the texts are concealed before Mañjuśrīmitra meets Śrī Siṃha, and that Śrī Siṃha only recovers the texts following the *parinirvāṇa* of Mañjuśrīmitra. Since Mañjuśrīmitra does not have the texts in hand, it is clear that the teaching Śrī Siṃha receives from Mañjuśrīmitra is the aural lineage teaching, presumably both written and unwritten. The same pattern repeats itself with Śrī Siṃha and Jñānasūtra. Between Jñānasūtra and Vimalamitra, Śrī Siṃha only entrusts the latter with the outer, inner, and secret cycles of the intimate instruction series, along with the aural lineages. However, Śrī Siṃha entrusts all four cycles of the intimate instruction series and the aural lineages to Jñānasūtra and reveals where the texts are concealed in eastern China. Jñānasūtra travels there to recover the texts and bestows the remaining instructions as well as the texts upon Vimalamitra. En route to Tibet, Vimalamitra conceals some texts in Kashmir,

20. *Precious Garland Chronicle*, p. 93.

and on arrival to Tibet entrusts both the explanatory and aural lineages to a single person, his principal disciple, Nyang Tingzin Zangpo. The *Mind Mirror of the Aural Lineage* notes:

> When Vimalamitra arrived, he taught many outer and inner dharmas. He examined who was a suitable recipient for this aural lineage. He went to Hepori,[21] observed Nyak Jñānakumara, and saw he was not a suitable recipient. Vimalamitra said to Nyang Tingzin Zangpo, "In general, gold is valued to the south of Nepal. In particular, the people of India value gold. After you have sold your entire estate, will you give your gold to me?"
>
> Nyang thought, "Since Vimalamitra didn't want the king or Nyak, but instead wants me, it is necessary to make an offering to gather accumulations."
>
> Since Vimalamitra knew Nyang's thoughts, he said, "I don't need gold. I was examining your suitability as a recipient, and you are a suitable recipient."
>
> Then, at that time, he taught Nyang the aural lineage.[22]

The significance of this is that Nyak Jñānakumara, an important translator during the eighth and ninth centuries, is someone through whom the Kham tradition of the mind series was transmitted. Here, he is considered an unsuitable recipient for the cittatilaka teachings in general. Moreover, the king too is excluded from receiving them, placing this narrative at variance with other narratives.

Longchenpa notes both in the *Precious Garland Chronicle* and the *Profound Mirror* that after Nyang conceals the texts of the intimate instruction series and entrusts them to the protector Vajrasādhu, he transmits the aural lineages that he has set down in notes to his principal student Bé Lödro Wangchuk. Bé transmits the aural lineage to Dromtön Rinchen Bar, who in turn transmits it to Dangma Lhungi Gyaltsen.

21. A tall hill overlooking Samyé Monastery.

22. See p. 105 in this volume.

At this time, Vajrasādhu reveals to Dangma where the texts are concealed. Dangma retrieves them, and thirty years later meets with a young man named Sengé Wangchuk, bequeathing both the aural and textual lineages.

Sengé Wangchuk then splits these two lineages again, teaching the textual lineage to his student, Chegom Nagpo, and entrusting the aural lineage to an obscure yogi named Shongpa Repa. The aural lineage is passed down through a number of masters, one-to-one, until it reaches Nyantön Sherab Tsemo, who releases the command seal, transmitting it to Yönten Gangpa. Permitted by his guru to spread the aural lineage more widely, Yönten Gangpa gives the transmission to Lama Namkha Dorjé, among others. The transmission is then received by Kumararāja, who in turn transmits it to Longchenpa. Finally, Longchenpa reunites the transmissions of the textual and aural lineages in the *Lama Yangtik* and *Zabmo Yangtik*.

Combining these two lineages evidently led to some apprehension among Longchenpa's contemporaries, as indicated by statements Longchenpa makes in the *Self-Appearing Direct Perception*. The importance of the relationship between the aural lineage and the cittatilaka tradition is explained as follows:

> One may think that since luminosity appears in actuality in this aural lineage, it is not the secret cycle. However, though it is nominally designated "the secret cycle," this is defined as the aural lineage to prevent the decline of the cittatilaka tradition. The *Great Chronicle* states that this was named the unwritten aural tradition "in order that the tradition not decline."[23]

Further, Longchenpa makes an important distinction in the *Self-Appearing Direct Perception* between the written and unwritten aural lineages:

23. See p. 74 in this volume.

> Since the unwritten aural lineage is abbreviated, it is designated the "secret cycle," because the major key points about the way the four visions arise, and so on, are absent. However, since this unwritten aural lineage explains pristine consciousness appearing to the eyes, it is superior to the written [aural lineage] because of the key points of the doors, and so on.[24]

The objection some might raise is that the aural lineage belongs to the secret cycle because the proof texts of the aural lineage depend completely upon tantras classified as belonging to the outer, inner, and secret cycles. Longchenpa responds to this by pointing out a key feature of the unwritten aural lineage that distinguishes it from other secret cycle aural lineages. When describing the explanatory lineages in more detail, Longchenpa states in the *Treasury of Siddhānta*:

> When divided, there are four: the outer cycle, inner cycle, secret cycle, and unsurpassed secret cycle. First, the essence of the outer cycle is employing the five poisons as the path, because afflictions do not exist to be abandoned. The nature of the outer cycle is whatever appears arises as dharmatā, because there is no accomplishment through effort. The characteristic of the outer cycle is that emptiness is completely undivided, because there are no distinctions.
>
> The essence of the inner cycle is the dharmatā without signs, because matter does not exist as an intrinsic characteristic. The nature of the inner cycle is that pristine consciousness always exists, because it neither comes nor goes. The characteristic of the inner cycle is that it occurs like a root from the perspective of penetrating, it is like a trunk from the perspective of concentricity, it is like a leaf from the perspective of spreading, it is like a flower from the perspective of clarity, and it is like a fruit from the perspective of ripening.

24. See p. 75 in this volume.

> The essence of the secret cycle is that there is no dependence on hearing, reflection, or meditation, because introduction and realization are obtained simultaneously. The nature of the secret cycle is that there is no dependence on the power of diligence or cultivation, because expiration and buddhahood are simultaneous. The characteristic of the secret cycle is that there is no dependence on completion of the two causal accumulations, because buddhahood and compassion are simultaneous.
>
> The essence of the unsurpassed secret cycle is that there is no dependence on an analytical consciousness, because there is no reliance on words. The nature of the unsurpassed secret cycle is that there is no dwelling in a view of intellectual grasping, because the view is known in direct perception. The characteristic of the unsurpassed secret cycle is that there are no expectations concerning the three kāyas and the five pristine consciousnesses of the result, because the measure of the fourth vision is reached.[25]

Unfortunately, when the *Treasury of Siddhānta* lists the catalog of Dzogchen tantras included in the intimate instruction series, it only lists the Seventeen Tantras and neglects to list the many tantras later editors of the Collected Tantras of the Ancient (NGB) included in the outer, inner, and secret cycles. The consequence of this is that our main sources for understanding the tantras of the secret cycle are the aural lineage texts presented by Longchenpa.

The main proof texts Longchenpa relies upon to validate the unwritten aural lineage are the *Compendium of Tilakas* (*Thig le 'dus pa*), the *Compendium of All Tilakas* (*Thig le kun 'dus*), and the *Universal Tilaka* (*Thig le kun gsal*), frequently referred to as the *Explanatory Tantra*. The presentation of these aural lineages offers some insight into how this large class of tantras was understood, since apart from the ancillary texts of the

25. *Treasury of Siddhānta*, pp. 1166–68.

Compendium of Tilakas, no extant commentaries are dedicated specifically to the tantras of the secret cycle.

The *Compendium of Tilakas* is a collection of texts that appear in the same order in both the Collection of Tantras of Vairocana (BGB) and the NGB. That the *Compendium of Tilakas* cycle appears in the same order in both the BGB and NGB points to its importance and the stability of its transmission. This cycle possesses a fundamental tantra followed by two supplemental tantras and a series of ancillary instructions. The first of these ancillary instructions, attributed to Garab Dorjé, is the *Precious Activity at the Time of Death* for benefiting others at the time of death. Following this is the aural lineage text by Sengé Wangchuk, the *Intimate Instruction of Samantabhadra Merging the Three Kāyas*, which he describes as the aural lineage of the *Compendium of Tilakas*. Next, another text called the *Precious Activity at the Time of Death* has a concise presentation of the death process. These two texts relating to death may in fact be part of one text, divided into respective sections. Following this is a text called the *Sole Unique Tilaka of Buddhahood*, which addresses the self-liberation of *nāḍīs*, *vāyus*, and *bindus*.[26] Finally is a text called the *Intimate Instruction of the Secret Cycle*, which consists of more detailed presentations of nāḍīs, vāyus, and bindus. An anonymous colophon states:

> The cycle of the texts of the aural lineage is all mothers and children of the Tilaka cycle and the intent of Ja Nyog.[27] The aural lineage that identifies pristine consciousness nakedly shows the tilaka. Both the textual lineage and the introductions of the aural lineage are the instruction given with complete texts

26. Nāḍīs are physical structures in the body, classically enumerated to be 72,000, which serve to convey vāyus and bindus. Vāyus, derived from breathing, have different functions, but they are considered to be the principle of motility or the air element in the body, which governs circulation, moving, talking, digestion, excretion, and sense perception. There are many different kinds of bindus, some subtle, others physical, which are moved by the vāyus within the structures of the nāḍīs.

27. This person remains unidentified at present.

> at the retreat of Pangchen Zholhag Dechen. If promulgated [improperly], one goes to vajra hell.[28]

As one can see in the translations presented below, the aural lineage introductions of luminosity are drawn from the *Universal Tilaka Tantra*, but the way they are presented and the way these introductions are contextualized is unique to the aural lineage. Other important texts that are regularly cited are the *Blazing Body of the Charnel Ground Tantra* and *Chanting the Names of Mañjuśrī*.

The Translations

The overall structure of the aural lineage texts is a division into two subjects: the practice for this life and the practice for the bardo. The two short aural lineage texts present the practice of the empty, nonarising vidyā for this life. The two medium-length aural lineage texts present the practice of the luminosity of vidyā in the bardo. The two long aural lineage texts provide a more detailed elucidation of the practice of the luminosity of vidyā in the bardo. In general, we can understand that the practice of empty vidyā corresponds to *trekchö*[29] and the practice of luminosity corresponds to *thögal*,[30] however, without the technical detail that accompanies these two phases of cittatilaka practice.

There are three texts from the *Lama Yangtik*, distinguished as the short, middle-length, and great aural lineages: the *Self-Appearing Pristine Consciousness*, *Self-Appearing Luminosity of the Bardo*, and *Self-*

28. Anonymous, *Intimate Instruction of the Secret Cycle*, pp. 302–3.

29. *Khregs chod*, a term with two main explanations. The first is that *khregs* refers to a bundle tied together by a cord, and *chod* is an intransitive verb meaning "to separate." The second is that *khregs* refers to something solid and hard, while *chod* is the imperative of the verb *gcod pa*, "to cut."

30. *Thod rgal*, a term with two main explanations. The first is that *thod pa* refers to the forehead and *rgal ba* means "beyond," referring to the area about a cubit beyond the brow where the visions of Great Perfection practice occur. The second is "crossing over," meaning that this practice enables one to rapidly cross over the paths and stages.

Appearing Direct Perception of the Definitive Meaning, respectively. These are the primary texts for the aural lineage.

The first, the *Self-Appearing Pristine Consciousness*, has three general topics: the lineage, the instructions that arise from that lineage, and an entrustment. The main body of the text is divided into two parts: the preliminary practices and the direct introduction. There are seven preliminary practices: (1) guru yoga, (2) maṇḍala offering, (3) Vajrasattva meditation and recitation, (4) the yoga of impermanence, (5) the yoga of the suffering of saṃsāra, (6) the yoga of bodhicitta, and (7) the yoga of the natural state. The seventh topic, the yoga of the natural state, follows the classical analysis of where the mind arises from, and so on. This text is the basic text for the practice of this life and presents the preliminaries in detail. The preliminaries are practiced for forty-nine days, thirty-five days, or twenty-one days. Following the preliminaries, there is the direct introduction to nonarising empty vidyā, which itself is divided into two topics: the introduction of self-abiding consciousness and the introduction of self-arising consciousness as great self-liberation.

Next, the *Self-Appearing Luminosity of the Bardo* presents the practice of luminosity in six bardos:[31] (1) introducing the bardo of reality, (2) practicing in the bardo of the samādhi of luminosity, (3) taking the measure of the bardo of the deluded vision of dreams, (4) reminder in the bardo of the time of death when the elements are disturbed, (5) seizing the throne in the bardo of naturally perfected dharmatā, and (6) transitioning from the bardo of existence. The *Self-Appearing Luminosity of the Bardo* also introduces the paracanonical scheme of the six lamps: (1) the lamp of the abiding basis, (2) the lamp of the fleshy heart, (3) the lamp of the smooth white nāḍī, (4) the lamp of the watery far-reaching lasso, (5) the lamp of the time of the bardo, and (6) the lamp of the final result.[32] Longchenpa details these six lamps in the *Ultimate Mirror of the Aural Lineage*, translated below.

31. The *Blazing Light of the Precious Gem Tantra* is the source for the six bardos. See p. 167 in this volume.

32. The first four lamps are listed in the same order as the six lamps mentioned in the

The third of the aural lineage texts presented in the *Lama Yangtik* is the *Self-Appearing Direct Perception of the Definitive Meaning*. It has three topics: (1) the confirmation of the basis, (2) the practice of the path, and (3) the manner of the liberation of the result. Topic 1 has four subtopics: (1) the reality of the original basis, (2) the way saṃsāra and nirvāṇa are produced, (3) the way the body of traces is formed, and (4) the locations of mind and pristine consciousness.

The third and fourth subtopics are of particular importance. A key point some have missed in their assessment of Great Perfection contemplative modalities is the extent to which they are not dependent on any sort of intellectual analysis but instead depend on a keen understanding of the formation of the body and the physiological relationship between mind (*sems*) and pristine consciousness (*ye shes*), which is the basis for differentiating them. In *Stainless Space*, Longchenpa observes:

> It is very important to distinguish mind and pristine consciousness, because all meditation is just that; all methods of purifying vāyu and vidyā are that; and in the end, at the time of liberation, vidyā is purified of all obscurations because it is purified of mind.
>
> Since those are not distinguished in the common vehicles, awakening will not be attained for eons or lifetimes. Since the uncommon vehicles instantly recognize the intrinsic state of dharmakāya beyond mind, purifying vāyu and vidyā in one lifetime is also a critical point of attaining buddhahood.[33]

While it is certainly the case that Longchenpa's analytical presentations of the distinction between mind and pristine consciousness are of inter-

Aural Lineage of Zhangzhung; the fifth and sixth lamps, however, are different. For more information about this tradition, see Achard, *The Six Lamps: Secret Dzogchen Instructions of the Bön Tradition* (Somerville, MA: Wisdom Publications, 2017).

33. *Stainless Space*, pp. 416–17.

est,[34] they are not of much value in understanding his approach to the yoga of the Great Perfection. *Stainless Space* again addresses the basis of distinguishing mind and pristine consciousness:

> The essence of mind is the radiance of vidyā mounted on the vāyu. The essence of vidyā is intrinsically clear without vāyu.[35]

This distinction between mind and pristine consciousness cannot be arrived at analytically; it can only be confirmed experientially on the basis of introduction. The reason for this, as presented here and below, is that the distinction between concepts and dharmatā, mind and vidyā, is made based on the anatomical structure of a human being, which must be pointed out by a teacher, rather than by analytical faculties. This is especially important since the experiential recognition of this distinction is critical in the practical application of the path of the Great Perfection, providing the basis for such statements like the following, found in *Buddhahood in This Life*:

> If it is objected, "If afflictions are liberated into dharmatā without antidotes, there is no need for purification on the path. Otherwise, liberation would require no effort," for what reason would those who do not understand be liberated? Asserting that those who understand are liberated merely by recognizing concepts as dharmatā is the fruit of one's wishes. As such, to recognize that concepts are dharmatā, the intimate instructions of the guru are important.[36]

34. For a lengthy presentation and analysis of this subject, see Higgins, *The Foundations of Classical Rdzogs Chen in Tibet* (Vienna: Arbeitskreis für Tibetische und Buddhistische Studien, Universität Wien, 2013). While Higgins draws from *Stainless Space* to provide an account of this physiological distinction, his focus is principally analytical rather than yogic.

35. *Stainless Space*, p. 415.

36. Malcolm Smith, *Buddhahood in This Life* (Somerville, MA: Wisdom Publications, 2017), p. 161.

How are concepts dharmatā? Concepts are just the potential (*rtsal*) of the radiance (*gdangs*) of vidyā. As the *Self-Appearing Direct Perception of the Definitive Meaning* states:

> Since the radiance of vidyā in the heart center is moved by the horse of the karma vāyu, its potential arises as concepts, arising as the path of deluded saṃsāra because of ignorance.[37]

Next, the *Self-Appearing Direct Perception of the Definitive Meaning* gives instructions on the practice for this life: practicing the intrinsic clarity of the mind without grasping and practicing pristine consciousness as naturally perfected luminosity. The text then moves on to the death process, discussing in detail three topics: (1) the preliminaries, the way the elements gather; (2) the main subject, the way pristine consciousness arises; and (3) the conclusion, the way of progressing to the buddhafields. Here, the process of liberation in the bardo is explained in detail. At the conclusion of the text the result is explained in terms of the three calibers of practitioners: best, middling, and average.

Next, we turn to the second volume of the *Zabmo Yangtik*, which is devoted solely to explaining the aural lineage. It is clear that long after he completed the *Lama Yangtik*, Longchenpa wrote the *Zabmo Yangtik* aural lineage texts to supplement and expand his earlier writing. Volume two of the *Zabmo Yangtik* begins with devotional supplications and a method of conferring the empowerment for the secret cycle. Following this is the *Great Guide for the Path of the Supreme Secret*, which is an outline of the *Self-Appearing Pristine Consciousness*. Next is a verse text, *Resting in Primordial Liberation*, a declaration of Longchenpa's realization of the Great Perfection teachings. Here, as in other texts, his mature skepticism toward philosophy and analysis is on display:

> How can dharmatā be realized by the vehicles of cause and
> result?

37. See p. 71 in this volume.

> Just as the childish argue about whether space exists or not,
> how can they reach the meaning nothing can be removed
> from or added to?
> Will analysis that depends on provisional and definitive texts
> ever see the reality of the essence that is free of proliferation?
> Will valid cognitions of direct perception and inference
> ever see the fundamental mind itself?
> While unaffected by the taints of beginningless traces,
> at present bound by the tethers of philosophical imputations,
> one is surrounded by a fence of traces, never free from
> the city of existence of the three realms and six classes of
> beings.
> Since it is difficult to completely cut through the web of
> concepts,
> how can people who have already cultivated this nature
> enter the true meaning of dharmatā?[38]

Next are the *Mind Mirror of the Aural Lineage* and the *Ultimate Mirror of the Aural Lineage*. The first section of the *Mind Mirror* presents a chronicle of the lineage, and the second section is divided into four topics: (1) the examination of the basis, the reality of the abiding basis; (2) the examination of delusion with regard to the path, the way delusion is deluded; (3) the examination of the instructions for the three grades of calibers, the method of reversing the delusion to be reversed; and (4) the examination of the six bardos, the way the liberated result is liberated. The first topic is a brief résumé of the nature of the basis and the liberation of Samantabhadra. The second topic describes how sentient beings become deluded. The third topic outlines the types of practitioners and how they are to be introduced to the teachings. The fourth topic briefly summarizes the six bardos, which are explained in detail in the *Self-Appearing Luminosity of the Bardo*.

Next is the *Ultimate Mirror*, the longest and most detailed of the texts translated here, nearly twice as long as the *Self-Appearing Direct*

38. See pp. 99–100 in this volume.

Perception of the Definitive Meaning. It also has three sections: (1) the chronicle of the lineage's source for confidence, (2) the intimate instruction of how the instruction is bestowed, and (3) the instruction concerning the introduction for realization and liberation. In the first section, which recounts the chronicle of the lineage, a nirmāṇakāya called Teacher Vajrasattva takes apparitional birth and receives introductions from the buddhas of the five families of the vajradhātu maṇḍala. In turn he emanates Garab Dorjé, and so on. Section two details the necessities of bestowing the aural lineage. Section three greatly expands upon the introductions first presented in the *Self-Appearing Luminosity of the Bardo*. It has five topics: (1) confirming the basis, path, and result; (2) binding the key points with the six lamps; (3) summarizing the essentials as pristine consciousness; (4) planting the nail with the five inscriptions; and (5) setting the command seal through high value. The last text in this collection is the *Essential Handbook*, which contains advice on postures, gazes, and breath.

The final and longest text in the second volume of the *Zabmo Yangtik* is the *Profound Mirror*, which is not translated here. It is my hope that I can present it as a follow-up volume in the future.

When reading texts of the Great Perfection, the reader must always keep in mind that they are not reading books of analytical philosophy—the Great Perfection cannot be understood in that way. These texts are principally manuals for practitioners who have received the proper transmissions. With respect to all publication of the Great Perfection texts, it may seem that its guardians have relaxed their watchful eye, but they have not. Therefore, it is quite important that the reader seek out the proper transmission for these teachings from a qualified teacher and apply them systematically. As it is often stated in Great Perfection texts, one should treat these texts as more valuable than one's eyes and heart.

In closing I would like to acknowledge my principal root guru, the second Vajrasattva, Chögyal Namkhai Norbu (1938–2018). He was the teacher from whom I learned the overall importance of the aural lineage traditions in the Great Perfection tradition and the unified meaning of the three series of the Great Perfection. I would also like to acknowledge the late Kunzang Dechen Lingpa (1928–2006), the guru from whom I received the *Fourfold Cittatilaka* empowerments and transmissions. A student of Dudjom Rinpoché, Kunzang Dechen Lingpa was a great yogi, treasure revealer, and model practitioner who dedicated his life to the practice of the Great Perfection. It is to his memory that we dedicate this translation. Next, I would like to thank Osa Karen Manell, principal editor of Zangthal Editions, whose keen eye and endless patience contributed immensely to the quality this book. I would also like to acknowledge Daniel Aitken and the staff at Wisdom Publications, without whom this and many other translations from Zangthal Editions would not have seen the light of day. And finally, I would like to thank the Zangthal Sangha, whose dedication to the Great Perfection tradition inspired us to translate these precious texts on their behalf.

Ācārya Malcolm Smith, Ashfield, MA

Self-Appearing Pristine Consciousness: The Short Aural Lineage

I pay homage to the guru who clearly explained
the meaning of the deep, vast, and unsurpassed essence.
Among the three aural lineages of the supreme secret tilaka,[39]
Self-Appearing Pristine Consciousness will be set forth as a
manual.

Among the three series of the Natural Great Perfection,
the intimate instructions series also has outer, inner, and
secret cycles.
I shall write down the practice of the unwritten aural lineage,
which arises from the direct perception of luminosity
connected with the cittatilaka.[40]{348}

In this topical manual of the secret tilaka of the pinnacle of all vehicles, there are three topics: (1) the chronicle of the lineage, (2) the instruction that arises from the lineage, and (3) setting the seal of the prized doctrine.

1. The Chronicle of the Lineage

First, the aural lineage was explained by Śrī Samantabhadra to Vajrasattva. The latter explained it to Ācārya Garab Dorjé, and the lineage

39. Tib. *Thig le.*

40. Tib. *Snying thig.*

continued through Mañjuśrīmitra, Śrī Siṃha, Jñānasūtra, Vimalamitra, Nyang Tingzin Zangpo, Bé Lödro Wangchuk, Dro Rinchen Bar, Netan Dangma Lhungyal, Chetsun Sengé Wangchuk, Shongpa Repa, Zabtön Chöbar, Dampa Gyerzhig, Nyantön Sherab Tsemo, the peerless Yönten Gang Tulku and his brother Guru Namkha Dorjé, the sublime guru Kumarāja, and finally, the latter bestowed the aural lineage upon Longchen Rabjam.

2. The Instruction That Arises from the Lineage

The instruction that arises from the lineage has three topics: (1) the preliminary practice; (2) the main subject, direct introduction; and (3) the conclusion, how to sustain the experience.

2.1 The Preliminary Practice

2.1.1 Guru Yoga

From the seven-part mind training, the first is training the mind on guru yoga to open the door of blessings. Be seated on a comfortable seat. Go for refuge and generate bodhicitta.

On the crown of one's head, in the center of a sun and a moon seat, is one's root guru [in their ordinary form], smiling beautifully, into whom dissolve all the lineage gurus. On the periphery, swirling with lights and light rays, imagine an ocean of buddhas, bodhisattvas, ḍākinīs, and oath-bound guardians. Make a mental prostration, present outer and inner offerings, and confess the misdeeds accumulated from beginningless time. Recite this verse, and so on:

> Precious guru, bless me to recognize my own mind essence.
> Bless me to destroy the delusion of self-grasping.
> Bless me so that luminosity arises from within.

Having offered supplications from the depth of one's heart, oneself and the guru melt into light. Rest for a moment in the state of nonduality.

Then dedicate in the manner of a dream or an illusion. The purpose is to attain supreme and common *siddhis* after blessings arise effortlessly.

2.1.2 *Maṇḍala Yoga*

Train the mind in maṇḍala yoga to perfect the two accumulations. One should wipe the maṇḍala plate three times, place a heap in the center, and imagine a cloud bank of gurus, buddhas, and so on, in the space in front of oneself. At the conclusion of placing five or seven heaps, place a heap of flowers in the center. Present this five times while imagining that all buddhafields adorned with Sumeru and the four continents are filled with various gems, medicines, scents, flowers, and grains. Recite this verse, and so on:

> This precious maṇḍala is offered as a cloud of Samantabhadra offerings
> composed of medicine, incense, flowers, and grains,
> filling the whole expanse of space.
> May the wealth of kings totally satisfy all migrating beings.

Finally, since one dedicates in the state of nonduality of the absence of both self and other, the two accumulations are completed, and the two siddhis are swiftly attained.

2.1.3 *Vajrasattva*

Train the mind with the yoga of Vajrasattva to purify obscurations. In an instant, on the center of a lotus and a moon seat, one becomes Vajrasattva, who is white, with one face and two hands, holding a vajra to the heart in the right hand and a bell to the hip in the left hand. One's feet are in *vajrāsana*. One is adorned with silks and jewels. On a moon in one's heart center is a thumb-sized, white vajra[41] marked with *hūṃ* at its center. Surrounding *hūṃ* is the one-hundred-syllable mantra. Its light,

41. A five-tined vajra.

which is yellowish white like a blazing lamp flame, purifies the obscurations of oneself and all sentient beings.

Oṃ vajrasatva samaya manupālaya vajrasatvatvenopatiṣṭha driḍho me bhava sutoṣyo me bhava supoṣyo me bhava anurakto me bhava sarvasiddhim me prayaccha sarvakarma sucame cittaṃ śriyaṃ kuru hūṃ ha ha ha ha ho bhagavān sarvatathāgata hridaya vajra ma me muñca vajrībhava mahāsamayasatva āḥ[42] {352}

After the mantra is recited as much as one can accomplish, all appearances gather into *hūṃ* in the heart center. *Hūṃ* is left in an objectless state. The dedication purifies the misdeeds and obscurations gathered during many hundreds of thousands of eons. All breaches are mended. The purpose of this is to realize the meaning of the mind essence.

2.1.4 The Yoga of Impermanence

Train the mind in the yoga of the impermanence of life with the forceful method of adjusting one's perspective. Reflect on the condition of impermanence: Outwardly the seasons change. Inwardly the body increases and decreases, day and night change moment by moment, the older generation is passed by the younger generation, and so on. Train one's perspective concerning the impermanence of one's life. Since there is no permanence whatsoever, the purpose is for diligence in the Dharma to arise, like a blazing fire.

2.1.5 The Yoga of the Suffering of Saṃsāra

Train the mind in the yoga of the suffering of saṃsāra to generate weariness with existence. Reflect on the suffering of beings in the hot and cold hells; the hunger and thirst of *pretas*; the exploitation of animals; the birth, aging, illness, and death of humans; the conflicts of *asuras*; and the death and fall of *devas*. {353} In the past, one has repeatedly

42. This mantra is presented as it is transliterated in Longchenpa's text.

experienced similar kinds of suffering in saṃsāra. One will necessarily experience suffering if one does not practice dharma now. Since one sincerely reflects, "All sentient beings abiding in the dungeon of the suffering of saṃsāra are totally confused," and since one is wearied by the suffering of saṃsāra, the purpose is to wholeheartedly accomplish liberation.

2.1.6 The Yoga of Bodhicitta

Train the mind in the yoga of bodhicitta to progress on the path of Mahāyāna. Reflect on the suffering and harm to sentient beings abiding in saṃsāra, beginning with one's parents. Thinking of one's parents, understand that only oneself can place them on the stage of buddhahood. Having thought, "May my virtue cause all sentient beings to be happy," meditate on love for those like one's parents, compassion that wishes them to be free of suffering, and the wish to place them in awakening. The purpose of that is to turn all actions into the path of Mahāyāna, destroy the great power of misdeeds, {354} accomplish a great wave of virtue, and so on.

2.1.7 The Yoga of the Natural State

Train the mind in the yoga of the natural state by investigating the meaning of the fundamental mind essence. What is the initial source of the present mentation (*dran rig*) arising as a diversity (*sna tshogs*)?[43] What is its producing agent? Where is it dwelling at present? What is the dwelling agent? To where does it depart in the end? What is the departing agent like?

Examine apparent objects for subtle particles. After the mind arises from an object, does it stay or go? Identify the entity by investigating the dwelling agent, a moment of one's mind—does it exist as a sign, mark, shape, or color? As nothing whatsoever can be found with a thorough

43. In Dzogchen texts, the manifold appearances in the mind are referred to as "the diversity."

investigation, the inexpressible, uniform state is called "the transcendent state of original purity's own place." Since from this point of view the essence was seen in actuality, the purpose is to realize one's own mind as empty and clear, after it is understood that all phenomena of the universe and beings, and saṃsāra and nirvāṇa, are unsupported and primordially liberated. {355} As such, since the mind training on the preliminaries is extremely important, it is best to seriously dedicate oneself with devotion and great diligence to each subject for seven days; otherwise, five days is medium, and three days is average.

2.2 The Main Subject, Direct Introduction

There are two topics in direct introduction: (1) introducing nonarising empty vidyā, and (2) introducing naturally perfected luminosity.

2.2.1 The Direct Introduction to Nonarising Empty Vidyā

There are four topics: (1) ascertaining the view, (2) practicing meditation, (3) removing danger with conduct, and (4) abandoning hope and fear in the result.

2.2.1.1 Ascertaining the View

One's empty and clear vidyā is free from the extremes of existence and nonexistence, cannot be found upon examination, is not established by a cause, and is beyond a basis of expressing whether it exists or not. Though it cannot be identified by saying it exists, saying it does not exist does not cause it to become an absolute nonexistent. [Vidyā] is cognizant, clear, immediate, and vivid. This ordinary consciousness abides in its own state, like space.

2.2.1.2 Practicing Meditation

For practicing meditation, there is (1) the introduction of self-abiding consciousness as unfabricated or unadulterated, and (2) the introduction of self-arising consciousness as great self-liberation. {356}

2.2.1.2.1 The Introduction of Self-Abiding Consciousness

Relax one's body and mind. To introduce the unceasing radiance of vidyā, which arises from within the state of the mind itself that lacks discursiveness, there are three examples, five natures, and four signs of heat.

The three examples: rest like a cloud without any support at all, either external, internal, or in-between. Since the discursive effort of conceptuality is interrupted, vidyā is entirely left in its own place, like interrupting the stream of a water mill. Since [vidyā's] own place is recognized to be one's essential reality (*gshis kyi gnas lugs*), rest without the burden of effort and practice, and hope and fear, like a man who has finished work.

The five natures: when resting like that, dwell in that state, maintain it with mindfulness, do not be moved by concepts, eliminate hope and fear, and annul lethargy or agitation.

The four signs of heat: Since one meditates in that way, one feels one has no body or mind. Having merged with space, one feels there is homogeneity. One cannot bear to be separate from the state of joy and bliss arising from samādhi. As there has never been fear of saṃsāra and hope for nirvāṇa or dualistic grasping, {357} one feels that the transcendent state of buddhahood has always existed in oneself. Even though one does not desire the qualities of the eyes—clairvoyance, the four bases of miracles, and so on—they arise.

2.2.1.2.2 The Introduction of the Self-Liberation of Self-Arising Consciousness

To introduce the self-liberation of self-arising consciousness, when resting in the single, limpid state (*ngang dwangs*), the immeasurable variety of concepts and mentation is introduced as self-arising and self-liberated. There are three examples, five natures, and four signs of heat.

The three examples: The limpid state arises from the play of the mind. "Resting like waves dissolving into a river" means that the limpid state arises from the play of the mind and play self-liberates within the mind itself. "Resting like ripples on water" refers to the self-liberation [of play] vanishing without a trace. "Resting like the coils of a snake" means that [play] self-liberates on its own.

The five natures: when resting like that, the arising [of the limpid state] is identified; there is no relation between concepts of before and after; [concepts] automatically vanish without a trace; [there is] unadulterated, pure clarity; and movement and stillness are nondual.

The four signs of heat from that meditation: Since concepts do not harm the stilled mind, conceptuality and nonconceptuality are the same. {358} Since the five poisons are purified as they arise, attachments are pacified, like space. Since whatever meets the mind is liberated without a trace, negative conditions are employed as the path. Since equipoise and post-equipoise merge impartially, meditation is like a flowing river.

2.2.1.3 Removing Danger with Conduct

There are two topics in removing danger with conduct: (1) when abiding in equipoise in the limpid state, train in relaxing the sixfold group, because appearances and mind are liberated without duality; and (2) since in post-equipoise appearances are understood to be false, apparent objects are liberated as false; thus, train in the eight examples of illusion.[44]

44. See Longchenpa, *Finding Rest in Illusion* (Boulder: Shambhala Publications), 2018.

The first (training in realizing the sixfold group) is when one meditates on the limpid state as liberated upon arising, because one's mind does not arise, the objects of the six senses that grasp to form, sound, scent, taste, touch, and phenomena revert on their own. This is the direct introduction to the absence of clinging to appearances in their own place. The second (the liberation of apparent objects as false) is understanding that whatever appears is an illusion, a dream, and so on.

As such, for conduct there are three examples: as consciousness does not grasp apparent objects, behave without grasping to any trace of whatever the mind meets, like a madman; behave without clinging to appearances, like an illusion; and behave without accepting and rejecting, and without hope and fear, like a small child. {359}

The five natures: appearing in aspects, not conceiving objects, direct elimination, lacking [both] accepting and rejecting, and not being caught up in conditions.

The four signs of heat: such conduct arises without focusing on appearances, desires are exhausted, proofs and refutations are destroyed, and never going beyond dharmatā.

2.2.1.4 Abandoning Hope and Fear in the Result

The introduction of the result, the self-liberation of one's vidyā: no matter how one meditates or investigates, the first moment of consciousness is liberated without a trace, impartially self-abiding.

The three examples: consciousness's own place is determined to be dharmakāya, confirmed like meeting a previous acquaintance; there is no need for effort or practice, confirmed like the nature of space; and the content of the mind arises as dharmatā, confirmed like a caravan leader staying at home after receiving jewels.

The five natures are abiding directly in liberation, lacking fabrication and adulteration, exhausting activities, naturally relaxed, and deeply blissful.

The four signs of the heat of experience: one is free from a mind that aspires for anything, doubts about what is and what is not are exhausted, one is never separate from boundless dharmatā, {360} and one is free from a mind that affirms hope and fear. These are the foundation for practice in this life.

2.2.2 The Introduction of Naturally Perfected Luminosity

The introduction of naturally perfected luminosity is (1) the original reality; (2) the way saṃsāra and nirvāṇa separated; (3) the way pristine consciousness dwells in the body; (4) the way that pristine consciousness is introduced as the three kāyas; (5) the way sound, light, and rays and the appearances of pristine consciousness arise in the bardo; and (6) the way the benefit of sentient beings is produced once there is liberation in the original result. [These] are introduced according to the middle-length and great aural lineage.

2.3 Post-Equipoise

How to maintain appearances in post-equipoise: having made effort in practicing according to the introductions—meditating without lethargy or agitation or becoming entangled in signs through grasping and becoming confident in the transcendent state of pristine consciousness abiding in oneself—thinking that there is another bardo, train in the bardo introductions in the four sessions of day and night and recall the instructions.

3. Setting the Seal of the Prized Doctrine

To set the seal of the prized doctrine, place an image of the *yidam* or a *torma* on the head [of the disciple] and make them promise, "Each day, in each session of practice, or even if not practicing, in the end I will show the example, words, and meanings of the instruction to others." This is also the tradition of entrusting benefit to the qualified recipient.

> As such, the meaning of the essence of the most secret aural lineage
> has been extracted and placed in the palm of the hand.

After fortunate migrating beings reach awakening,
may everything be pacified, and may buddhahood be
accomplished.

The cittatilaka of Vimalamitra, *Self-Appearing Pristine Consciousness*, the concise aural lineage from the supreme secret tilaka, was completed by Longchenpa, the yogi of the supreme vehicle, on the slopes of Gangri Thökar.

Self-Appearing Luminosity of the Bardo: The Middle-Length Aural Lineage

I pay homage to the feet of the sublime guru
who shows the meaning of the essence of luminous pristine consciousness.
Listen with devotion to the explanation of this aural lineage of
the self-appearing luminosity of the bardo for the benefit of future generations.

Now then, though there are many divisions of the bardos, here there are six: (1) introducing the bardo of reality, (2) practicing in the bardo of the samādhi of luminosity, (3) taking the measure with the bardo of the deluded vision of dreams, (4) reminder in the bardo of the time of death when the elements are disturbed, (5) seizing the throne in the bardo of naturally perfected dharmatā, and (6) transitioning from the bardo of existence.

1. *Introducing the Bardo of Reality*

The first topic, introducing the bardo of reality, has three sections: (1) identifying the topic, (2) demonstrating the signs, and (3) generating confidence through examples.

1.1 Identifying the Topic

The pristine consciousness of vidyā is the most refined pure essence within the nāḍī of the pristine consciousness of luminosity in one's heart center, like a wick. The empty essence, the dharmakāya, is free from all extremes of proliferation, like space. The clear nature, the saṃbhogakāya, appears like a rainbow. The entity of cognizance, natureless compassion, the nirmāṇakāya, is like the surface of a mirror. The kāyas and pristine consciousnesses exist inseparably as innate attributes of the transcendent state.

1.2 Demonstrating the Signs

The heart center is connected to the eyes by the crystal tube, the nāḍī of light. Just as in the illustration of light shining from a lamp, {363} the light of the empty bindu arises from the illustrated luminous pristine consciousness that exists within.

1.3 Generating Confidence through Examples

Though the empty essence, clear nature, and unceasing compassion can each be illustrated with all kinds of individual examples of the inseparability of the three kāyas, to show this very clearly, there are four examples to be known when all [three kāyas] are introduced in the nature, with three topics each.

1.3.1 Introducing the Dharmakāya

At the time the dharmakāya is illustrated as empty, clear, and untainted through the example of a crystal, recite:

> A crystal displays light when the sun rises. Just as this crystal is immaculate and pellucid, vidyā also is immaculate and pellucid. Just as this crystal cannot be identified by any essential color, there is no essence to identify in vidyā. Just as

> this crystal has always been naturally lustrous even though it lacks substantial light, though the lights, kāyas, colors, and pristine consciousnesses are not established in the empty aspect of vidyā, its limpid state is the inseparable kāyas and pristine consciousnesses.

Having recited this, hold the crystal in the direction of the sun. The five lights[45] are clarity, the example of the saṃbhogakāya. {364} The white luster is compassion, cognizance, the example of the nirmāṇakāya. The pure essence is emptiness, the example of the dharmakāya. Just as these arise from the structure (*ngang*) of the crystal, exist in the structure of the crystal, and gather back into the structure of the crystal, introduce the kāyas and pristine consciousnesses arising from the essence—the state of the dharmakāya—dwelling in that state, and gathering back into that state.

1.3.2 Introducing the Saṃbhogakāya

To introduce the saṃbhogakāya through the example of a mask, the guru wears the accouterments of the saṃbhogakāya. Because the disciple looks at the guru through the Vajrasattva mirror, the outer expanse of space is filled with the appearance of the saṃbhogakāya.

> Just as the unimpeded appearance of the five lights is clear in this mirror, likewise, the kāyas and pristine consciousnesses exist in the dimension of luminosity. Because the crystal has no essence or nature, its pellucidity is the example of the dharmakāya. The appearance manifesting as kāyas and pristine consciousnesses is the example of the saṃbhogakāya. The explanation of the Dharma, and so on, arising as the aspect of vidyā is the example of the nirmāṇakāya. Since those are included in the single basis, they are inseparable.

45. For a comprehensive description of the five lights, see Malcolm Smith, *The Self-Arisen Vidyā Tantra: A Translation of the Rigpa Rangshar* (Somerville, MA: Wisdom Publications, 2018), pp. 127–29.

1.3.3 *Introducing the Nirmāṇakāya*

To introduce the example of the nirmāṇakāya, the union of the house of light, when the mirror is held up to the sun, the five lights appear without impediment: {365}

> Just as the five lights appear inside this crystal, one must understand that the radiance or potential of compassion of the nirmāṇakāya, which arises from the saṃbhogakāya, arises without impediment. Also, the empty, pellucid aspect is the example of the dharmakāya. The appearance of the five lights is the example of the saṃbhogakāya. The rays arising from the crystal are the example of the nirmāṇakāya. Those three are inseparable in a single nature. Alternatively, when the crystal is held up to a lamp, the transparent appearance is the example of the dharmakāya. The lamp as the basis is the example of the saṃbhogakāya. The light spreading from that lamp appearing in space is the example of emanations in the ten directions.

Those are introduced as inseparable by nature in a single basis.

1.3.4 *Introducing the Inseparable Three Kāyas*

The nonconceptual nature of the sun is the example of the dharmakāya. The sun's brilliant, radiant appearance of five lights is the example of the saṃbhogakāya. The sun's effulgent rays are the example of the nirmāṇakāya. Those three included in one sun are the example of the inseparability of the kāyas and pristine consciousnesses. The *Universal Tilaka* states: {366}

> The luminosity in the dimension of mind
> resembles a lamp in a vase.
> Unchanging pristine consciousness
> is the buddhahood of the undeluded basis,

the sublime meaning pristine consciousness.
The mirror of great pristine consciousness
is the unfabricated dharmatā,
the sublime example pristine consciousness.
The maṇḍala of light, which is the size of one's thumb,
is explained to be the proof pristine consciousness.[46]

2. Practicing in the Bardo of the Samādhi of Luminosity

There are three topics for practicing in the bardo of the samādhi of luminosity: (1) meditating on the meaning pristine consciousness during the day, (2) meditating on the proof pristine consciousness during the night, and (3) meditating on the example pristine consciousness between sessions.

2.1 Meditating on the Meaning Pristine Consciousness During the Day

To meditate on the meaning pristine consciousness during the day, sit in an upright posture with both arms crossed above the knees. Since one gazes with the eyes at an arrow's length in distance and meditates by focusing the mind without distraction, one sees the appearance of light in various patterns of rainbows and nets of bindus. Since internally the mind meditates on the state of the arising pristine consciousness that is clear, radiant, and nonconceptual, the experience and realization of bliss, clarity, and nonconceptuality will arise.

2.2 Meditating on the Proof Pristine Consciousness During the Night

To meditate on the proof pristine consciousness during the night, be seated as before, cover the eyes with the fingers, and press gently on the eyeballs. Since one meditates looking directly at the empty bindu, {377}

46. Unattested.

externally the appearance of light arises as a diversity, and internally the experience of the concentration of bliss, clarity, and nonconceptuality arises as before.

2.3 Meditating on the Example Pristine Consciousness Between Sessions

To meditate on the example pristine consciousness between sessions, determine that the three kāyas are innate attributes with either a crystal, an image of a deity, or the sun. In a state of thinking that this is the bardo's own appearance, since one rests directly in the recognition of the bardo's own appearance, the intention is to easily recognize the moment of arising in the bardo. Also, since the appearance is recognized as the three kāyas, various outer and inner experiences arise such as the arising of the buddhafield of great bliss as an appearance, and so on. Thus, if one makes effort in these three practices, undoubtedly the best will be liberated in this life.

3. Taking the Measure of the Bardo of Dreams

To take the measure of the bardo of dreams, when the time comes to increase good and bad dreams, as a sign of thinning the traces of delusion of daytime appearances through such practice, one merges positive and negative traces. Though at that time the afflictions of the mind {368} are reduced, if one dies at that time, there is a remainder for the bardo of rebirth.

Next, when one dreams only positive dreams, at that time virtue becomes one taste through the exhaustion of positive and negative karma. Since there is no positive or negative karma, after dreams diminish, there are no dreams in the end. At that time, since the diminishment of traces and afflictions as the measure of dissolution into the *dhātu* is reached, there isn't a speck of dualistic grasping in one's mind. When one masters the meditation of the mind, expiration and liberation occur simultaneously. If one becomes very familiar, since the body transforms into light, there are no remaining aggregates in this life, which is the measure of perfect [buddhahood].

4. Reminder in the Bardo of the Time of Death When the Elements Are Disturbed

To be given a reminder in the bardo of the time of death when the elements are disturbed, at the time the elements gather, one's guru or a *samaya* sibling reminds one of the bardo advice. Otherwise, one recalls it and remains undistracted.

Now, for the way the elements gather, since the vāyu of earth dissipates into water, the body becomes heavy. Since the vāyu of water dissipates into fire, the mouth and nostrils become dry. {369} Since the vāyu of fire dissipates into air, warmth gathers from the extremities. Since the vāyu of air dissipates into space, at that time blood gathers into the heart center from inside the life nāḍī (aorta), which is called "The king is seated on the throne and defended by the minister." Once there is an exhalation with *ha*, since one cannot inhale, "the mind dissipates into space," and the time approaches when vidyā is expelled from within the heart center.

5. Seizing the Throne in the Bardo of Naturally Perfected Dharmatā

Seizing the throne of naturally perfected dharmatā has three topics: (1) divisions of the bardo, (2) the way the instruction is demonstrated, and (3) the mode of liberation of the result.

5.1 Divisions of the Bardo

5.1.1 The Best

Among the three in this topic, the mode of liberation in the natural bardo is for those of the highest caliber. The best of the highest caliber are liberated through introduction. The introduction and liberation are simultaneous, realization and abandoning the Dharma are simultaneous, abandoning the Dharma and the cessation of deluded concepts are simultaneous, the cessation of deluded concepts and the clearing away of ignorance are simultaneous, clearing away ignorance and expanding pristine consciousness are simultaneous, and expanding pristine consciousness and full buddhahood are simultaneous. Therefore, when an uncommon, confident realization arises in one's continuum, {370} it is liberation because saṃsāra is never entered.

The middling of the highest are liberated by practice. Their practice relies on the radiant light that arises through the connection between the heart center and the eyes, and they see the maṇḍala of luminosity. Since they are liberated into the inseparable three kāyas, the bardo does not appear.

The average of the highest are liberated by direct recognition and cast off the body. Just as there is no period of darkness on the fifteenth day of the month when the sun sets and the moon rises, likewise, when the appearances of this life subside through the gathering of the elements, both the vidyā that emerges from the heart center through the water lamp and the appearance of pristine consciousness penetrate space, like many colors intertwined (*snye tshon sgril ba*). Since one recognizes this, one is liberated instantly into the pellucidity above, and there is no bardo.

5.1.2 The Middling

Among those of middling caliber who are liberated in the bardo of dharmatā, the best of the middling are liberated in three instants: The instant of stirring up saṃsāra from the bottom occurs after all delusion—appearing as the outer universe and inner beings—ceases, and one's radiance then manifests as light. The instant of seeing the truth of dharmatā is the arising of a consciousness free of grasping the intrinsically clear maṇḍala of clusters. The vajra-like instant occurs when, having obtained one's own benefit, the dharmakāya, {371} the benefit of others is produced, the *rūpakāya*. Further, in the first instant pristine consciousness arises. In the second instant one recognizes pristine consciousness as the instruction of the guru. In the third instant the benefit of beings is produced, because one's realization merges evenly with the buddhas of the past.

For the middling of the middling who are liberated in six instants, in the first instant outer and inner delusions such as earth, stones, mountains, cliffs, and so on, cease. In the second instant one's radiance manifests as light. In the third instant one abides in the state of reality (*de nyid*). In the fourth instant certainty arises within oneself. In the fifth instant the fivefold transcendent state is complete. In the sixth instant there is dissolution into the dharmakāya beyond thought when the three kāyas are taken as one's own place.

5.1.3 *The Average*

The average of the middling are liberated on the fifth day of concentration. The outer elements cease, appearing like the setting sun. The inner elements—the sixfold group—cease like dusk. The secret elements—the appearance of the kāyas and pristine consciousnesses—manifest simultaneously like the rising moon. Since the samādhi of realization arises gradually, there is liberation in the cluster of the five families. Further, since the blue light is recognized as the pristine consciousness of the dharmadhātu, one is liberated as Vairocana and attains buddhahood {372} in the cluster of the five families. Since the white light is recognized as the mirror-like pristine consciousness, one is liberated as Akṣobhya. Since the yellow light is recognized as the pristine consciousness of uniformity, one is liberated as Ratnasambhava. Since the red light is recognized as the individually discerning pristine consciousness, one is liberated as Amitābha. Since the green light is recognized as the successful activity pristine consciousness, one is liberated as the maṇḍala of the Amoghasiddhi couple. Further, the five families do not arise sequentially; rather, they arise simultaneously, manifesting as the luminosity of the heart center. The individually ascertaining wisdom arises gradually. At the same time there is no grasping to objects, because there is not a moment of mind. The *Universal Tilaka* states:

> The appearances of luminosity arise immediately.
> The wisdom of realization arises gradually.[47]

Also, a concentration day is held to be the duration of stable equipoise in samādhi.

5.2 *The Way the Instruction Is Demonstrated*

The way the instruction is demonstrated: Just as one remains in a state of certainty through recognition, like meeting a previous acquaintance, the luminosity of the bardo is also said to exist as an innate attribute once it has been introduced by the guru. Here, confidence is recognition simultaneous with its arising. {373} Since there is uniform equipoise in a state of certainty without adulterating fabrications, one abides for an instant in samādhi. At that time one is liberated.

5.3 *The Way the Result Is Liberated*

For the way the result is liberated, as such, in whichever way one is liberated, after the six higher perceptions arise, there is liberation in the precious, naturally perfect, original dhātu, the buddhafield of the youthful vase body, the uninterrupted ornamental wheel of body, speech, and mind. Above, the higher perception of the eye sees the buddhafield of the dharmakāya beyond mind; in front, it sees the saṃbhogakāya; and below, it sees the individual deeds of the nirmāṇakāya. Above, the higher perception of the ear hears the unwavering speech of the dharmakāya; in front, it hears the saṃbhogakāya; and below, it also hears the language of the nirmāṇakāyas of the six realms. Above, the higher perception of mind knows that the dhātu and vidyā are inseparable, the transcendent state of the dharmakāya; in front, it knows the saṃbhoga-

47. This citation appears to be an adaptation of a passage in UT, p. 459: */ye shes kyi gdangs la zhig ngar gnas te shar cig char shar ro/ de yang ye shes kyi snang ban am mkha' la 'jah shar ba ltar snang ngo/ de la rtogs pa'i shes rab rim pas skyes ste/ shag dang po mthing kar gsal bas rig pa ngos gzungs dang bral bac hos kyi dying kyi ye shes/.* The passage goes on to recount the process of the arising of pristine consciousness in the order given here.

kāya; and below, it knows the transcendent state of the nirmāṇakāya. Above, higher perception of place knows the place where the dharmakāya abides; in front, it knows the place where the saṃbhogakāya abides; and below, it knows the place where the nirmāṇakāya abides. The higher perception of karma {374} knows all natural causes and results. The higher perception of the four bases of magic power tames migrating beings with the six munis.

Rays of light shine from the tongues of the saṃbhogakāya couple and enter the eyes of a sublime person of pure karma. The rays of light enter the mouth of the mother from the father and enter the space of the mother from the vajra vase of the father's secret place, becoming a nirmāṇakāya from its coiling in the lotus pool, arising to tame any sentient being to be tamed.

Next, when dwelling in great, naturally perfected, inner clarity within the buddhafield of the youthful vase body, (1) wisdom lifts into space, (2) the elements subside into the mother, (3) pristine consciousness dissolves into the dhātu, (4) wisdom gathers in space, and (5) vidyā takes its own place.

5.3.1 Wisdom Lifts into Space

There are four in the first (wisdom lifts into space): (1) Powerful (*stobs ldan ma*), (2) Keeper of Power (*shugs 'chang ma*), (3) Lifter (*'degs byed ma*), and (4) Stabilizer (*brtan ma*).[48] The first nondually unites the principal and retinue. The second generates the state of dharmakāya in a single instant. The third always supports the rūpakāya in the state of the dharmakāya. The fourth naturally clarifies the unchanging transcendent state. {375}

48. These four female names indicate the personification of wisdom as an active principle in awakening. Longchenpa presents a slightly different set in the *Great Aural Lineage*.

5.3.2 The Elements Subside into the Mother

Since the impure elements are liberated into the pure elements, they abide as the characteristics of the five pristine consciousnesses. Further, air is well arrayed as a crossed vajra. Since the samaya goddess gathers into space, without moving, air dissolves into the dhātu. Earth is recognized as a smooth stūpa composed of the five kinds of gems in the manner of a tree. Without hardness, earth dissolves into the dhātu. Fire is a brilliant web of lotuses, ripening the unripened. Without heat, fire dissolves into the dhātu. Water collects into a single pure pristine consciousness, dissolving the appearance of impure delusion into pure dharmatā. Without moisture, water dissolves into the dhātu.

5.3.3 Pristine Consciousness Dissolves into the Dhātu

Since exteriorized clarity—the pristine consciousness of the omniscience of all aspects—dissolves into interiorized clarity—the pristine consciousness of omniscience—clarity is intrinsically clear in the state of nonconceptuality.

5.3.4 Wisdom Gathers in Space

At that time, (1) [pristine consciousness] has dissolved, but is not hazy; (2) it is clear, but is not conceptual; (3) it exists, but without a self; and (4) it is differentiated, but not separated.

First, when pristine consciousness dissolves into the dhatu, {376} it abides as interiorized clarity, like the new moon. Second, though the kāyas and pristine consciousnesses exist as the appearance of the five lights, there is no conceptual clinging. Third, although self-originated pristine consciousness exists, it lacks "I" and "mine." Fourth, although the unceasing appearance of the kāyas and pristine consciousnesses are individually and unceasingly distinct, since the essence is inseparable, there is no differentiation into separate substances.

5.3.5 Vidyā Takes Its Own Place

Because the dharmakāya is immutable, it is a kāya, like a vajra. Because pristine consciousness is unceasing, it is longevity, like a swastika. Since samādhi is uninterrupted, it is a continuum, like a river. Since the transcendent state lacks clarification and obscuration, it exists like the heart of the sun. These constitute the brief explanation of the nascent state of liberation.

6. Transitioning from the Bardo of Karmic Existence

Transitioning from the bardo of karmic existence is the intimate instruction for one of excellent karma transitioning from the bardo of existence, like repairing an irrigation canal. Having previously not recognized the appearances of luminosity, once the consciousness leaves the body, {377} it enters into various lands, ephemeral and evanescent like a dream. Because one can travel without being impeded by anything, one is endowed with a magical base of karma. One cannot be seen by anyone apart from other bardo beings or those who possess the deva eye. At that time, one feels inherently cold, and one is unhappy. One's consciousness becomes seven times clearer than before. At that time, since one recognizes the bardo of death, it is explained that one recalls the guru and the instruction. Now, the best of the average recognize that all phenomena are false. The middling of the average avert the extreme of saṃsāra with the illusory creation and completion stages. The average of the average think either of the buddhafields of the five families, the pure buddhafield, the pledged deity, or the guru. Having gone for refuge, they turn away from saṃsāra and are born in the buddhafields. Also, the lowest of the average individual will shut the door to the lower realms through the traces left by the instructions and be reborn as a child with the eighteen freedoms and endowments into a family with faithful parents. Later, in twenty-five to thirty-five years, after they meet with this dharma, they will be liberated without the bardo. {378} This concludes the extensive explanation.

When those six topics are summarized, they are included in six lamps: (1) The lamp of the abiding basis is the luminous mind essence. (2) The lamp of the fleshy heart is the precious heart center, resembling a maroon tent. Within it, luminosity exists like a lamp inside a vase. (3) The lamp of the smooth white nāḍī is the path of luminosity. It is the nāḍī that connects the heart center to the eyes, like light through a skylight. (4) The lamp of the watery far-reaching lasso—the eyeballs of the two eyes—is the doorway of luminosity. (5) The lamp of the time of the bardo carries one to the original place, because appearances are recognized as the maṇḍala of luminosity. (6) The lamp of the final result takes the throne in the buddhafield of the youthful vase body, because pristine consciousness gathers into the dhātu.

Also, when those are summarized, they can be included in five topics: (1) the aggregate of the body is completely cast off, (2) conceptual movement ceases by vanishing, (3) the self-appearing maṇḍala arises instantly, (4) self-originated pristine consciousness is known vividly, and (5) original reality is liberated completely. {380}

> As such, the essential meaning, the culmination of all
> Dharmas,
> the profound, precise key point of luminosity
> is unlike anything, superior to all.
> Whoever attains this will cross the ocean of existence. {379}
> Thus, since a Dharma such as this is extremely rare,
> it must be diligently practiced by the fortunate one.
> Having liberated all migrating beings with this virtue,
> may they be effortlessly victorious on the original stage.

The *Self-Appearing Luminosity of the Bardo* from the supreme secret tilaka of the middle-length aural lineage was clearly set out by Longchen Rabjam, the yogi of the supreme vehicle, for the benefit of later generations.

This is protected by the Mistress of Mantra! Samaya.

Self-Appearing Direct Perception of the Definitive Meaning: The Great Aural Lineage

Homage to the sublime guru.

There are three in the practice of the key point of the immaculate mind essence, the meaning of the ultimate vehicle of the vajra essence: (1) the confirmation of the basis, (2) the practice of the path, and (3) the way of liberation of the result.

1. The Confirmation of the Basis

There are four in the confirmation of the basis: {380} (1) the reality of the original basis, (2) the way saṃsāra and nirvāṇa are produced, (3) the way the body of traces is formed, and (4) the locations of mind and pristine consciousness.

1.1 The Reality of the Original Basis

Prior to the establishment of either saṃsāra or nirvāṇa, the dharmadhātu—the empty, clear, unceasing essence—existed as the great source of the inseparable three kāyas. The empty essence is like space; the clear nature is like the sun and moon; and the radiance of compassion is like the surface of a polished mirror, a naturally undifferentiated nature that is a great reality without sameness or difference. If realized, this is the basis of the liberation of nirvāṇa. If not realized, this is the basis of saṃsāra. The *Epitome of Secrets* states:

Prior to production or arising,
the original protector Changeless Light
abides as the great source of everything.[49]

That is the demonstration of the sublime luminosity of the mind, the so-called *sugatagarbha*.

1.2 The Way Saṃsāra and Nirvāṇa Are Produced

Among the topics in the way saṃsāra and nirvāṇa are produced is the way Samantabhadra is liberated upon arising from the state of the original basis. Space was opened by the empty essence. The clear nature {381} self-arose as the naturally perfected five lights, the condition of apparent objects. When the radiance of the cognizance of compassion—the investigative consciousness—self-originated, Samantabhadra recognized his own light as arising naturally perfected from the beginning, like the reflection of a face arising in the mirror appearing as one's appearance. He was self-liberated at the beginning in a single instant. The *Tantra of Gathering the Definitive Meaning* states:

Because recognition was simultaneous
with the self-appearance of the self-originated maṇḍala,
the connate pristine consciousness arose,
and there was liberation on the intrinsically clear, original
stage.[50]

Chanting the Names of Mañjuśrī states:

Differentiated in a single instant,
in one instant, perfect buddhahood.[51]

49. The *Epitome of Secrets*, p. 617, which is found in the same volume as UT.

50. Unattested and incorrectly attributed to the *Tantra of Gathering the Definitive Meaning*. In the *Ultimate Mirror of the Aural Lineage* from the *Zabmo Yangtik*, Longchenpa attributes it to the *Universal Tilaka* with a slightly different ending; however, this is also unattested.

51. CNMa, 7b.

The way saṃsāra is produced: Since one does not recognize the self-appearance that arises from the basis, the connate ignorance is rendered a cause. Since the appearance that arises from oneself is apprehended as other, the imputing ignorance is rendered a condition. First, there is no form, then there is form, and thereafter, due to desire, gradually there is delusion. The *Universal Tilaka* states:

> The nonrecognition of one's state that is simultaneous with
> the self-appearance of the self-originated maṇḍala {382}
> produces the connate ignorance.
> Apprehending [the appearance] arising from oneself as other
> [than oneself]
> produces the imputing ignorance.
> The delusion of the three realms of existence arises from
> that.[52]

When space is opened by the empty essence, dharmatā is the basis of the delusion of objects. The appearance of the five lights is the basis of the delusion of the outer universe and also the basis of the delusion of the physical body. Cognizance (*rig pa*), the radiance of compassion, is the basis of the delusion of mind (*sems*). The *Universal Tilaka* states:

> Three bases of delusion arise from that:
> dharmatā is the basis of delusion of the object,
> the five lights are the basis of delusion of the body,
> and cognizance is the basis of delusion of the mind.
> Dharmatā is a valid basis of delusion of the object,
> because it is analogous to insentient[53] emptiness.
> The five lights are valid as the basis of delusion of the body,
> because they are analogous to the appearance of color.
> Cognizance is a valid basis of delusion of the mind,
> because it is analogous to the knowing of a mere knower.[54]

52. Unattested.

53. Reading *rig med* for *rigs med*.

54. See UT, p. 325, for a variant reading of this passage.

1.3 The Way the Body of Traces Is Formed

The beings of the formless realm have samādhi bodies, the four aggregates of name, which support their mental continuums. {383} The beings of the form realm have bodies composed of five lights, which support their mental continuums. The beings of the desire realm have bodies of physical flesh and blood, which support their mental continuums. Their bardo of transmigration in existence is a dream-like body of mental traces.

Among those [beings of the three realms,] the way the human is formed is described in the *Universal Tilaka*:

> Initially, the formation of the body begins with the eyes.
> From the connection of the two eyes to the navel,
> a knot of nāḍīs arises,
> from which the shape of body arises.[55]

During the first week, the oval *arbuda* (*mer mer po*),[56] which is one-third the size of a mustard seed, forms from the combination of four things: the white bindu of the father, the red bindu of the mother, and the vāyu and the mind of a gandharva who enters from the bardo seeking a body. A triangular cluster of nāḍīs forms in the middle of the *arbuda*. Two tiny eyes form in the center of the cluster.

During the second week, four nāḍī petals form in the four directions, which arise from the nāḍī that supports luminosity in the core of the oblong *kalala* (*nur nur po*). The pure part of blood, the size of one-hundredth of a horsehair, forms in the eastern nāḍī.

During the third week, {384} the pure part of flesh forms in the southern nāḍī of the lumpy *peśī* (*ltar ltar po*).

55. This is a paraphrase of a passage, UT, p. 442: */dang po bag chags lus 'di la /brtags nas srid pa'i cha bzung ba'o/de nas lus byin bskyed pa'o /mig gnyis dag nas rtsa gnyis shar te/de rtsa'i mdud pa gyur pas/de la lus gzhan bskyed pa rtsa'i yan lag rnams shar ro/.*

56. *Arbuda, kalala, peśī, ghana,* and *khara* are Ayurvedic terms describing the stages of the formation of the human embryo. For a more detailed presentation of these stages, see Malcolm Smith, *The Blazing Lamp Tantra and the Threaded String of Pearls* (Somerville, MA: Wisdom Publications), pp. 140–46.

During the fourth week, the pure part of heat forms in the western nāḍī of the round *ghana* (*gor gor po*).

During the fifth week, the pure part of breath forms in the northern nāḍī of the hardened *khara* (*'khrang gyur*). Further, though space is all-pervading, here space is located in the empty cavity of the central nāḍī. Thus, the action of the pure part of the five elements of the body supports all generation, preservation, and destruction of the body, and it also supports the five vāyus, the five afflictions, and the five pristine consciousnesses.

During the sixth week, the three main nāḍīs and four *cakra*s form in the center of the Viṣṇu tadpole. Further, in the manner of pillars, the central nāḍī is blue, the right *rasanā* is white, and the left *lalanā* is red.[57] An interconnected network of a set of four cakras splits off from these three main nāḍīs. These nāḍīs of the four cakras, which circle to the right, form the inner and outer petals of the body. The *mahāsukha* cakra[58] of the crown has thirty-two nāḍī petals, the *saṃbhoga* cakra of the throat has sixteen nāḍī petals, the *dharma* cakra of the heart center has eight nāḍī petals, and the *nirmāṇa* cakra of the navel has sixty-four nāḍī petals. The *Universal Tilaka* states:

> Though the four cakras of the nāḍī knots of the body {385}
> have many connections, like a network of wheels,
> the three nāḍīs of pristine consciousness that generate the
> three kāyas
> are supremely straight, like pillars in the body.[59]

Since *oṃ*, *āḥ*, and *hūṃ* abide inside those three nāḍīs, the karma of the three realms is accumulated. At the time of impurity, they act as

57. For a detailed presentation of the nature and function of these nāḍīs and cakras and their role in gestation, see Smith, *The Blazing Lamp Tantra and the Threaded String of Pearls*, pp. 161–66.

58. The *mahāsukha* cakra, the cakra of great bliss, is the seat of the sense perceptions of the five physical senses.

59. Unattested. This passage is attributed to Vimalamitra in Nyima Bum, *Eleven Topics of the Great Perfection* (Lhasa: Bod ljongs mi dmangs dpe skrun khang, 2008), p. 67, and Smith, *Buddhahood in This Life*, p. 105.

the support for the three doors and three poisons. At the time of purity, they act as the support for the three kāyas.

Clarity—the method—is generated from hatred through the *rasanā*. Bliss—wisdom—is perfected from desire through the *lalanā*. Nonconceptuality—the basis for the arising of the nondual pristine consciousness of union—arises from ignorance through the *avadhūti*.[60]

The four cakras act as the support for the four kāyas and the five pristine consciousnesses. In the center of those cakras are the syllables of the purifying pristine consciousnesses: *oṃ, āḥ, hūṃ, svā,* and *hā*. *Oṃ* is located in the crown, *āḥ* is located in the throat, *hūṃ* is located in the heart center, *svā* is located in the navel, and because there are five when the bliss-sustaining cakra of the groin is included, there is *hā*.

There are also three kinds of vāyu in those nāḍīs [of the Viṣṇu tadpole]: the primary vāyus, the secondary vāyus, and the vāyus that perform actions. First, in the four nāḍīs and in the center of the nāḍīs of the heart center {386} are the life-sustaining (*prāṇa*) vāyu in the center, the pervading vāyu in the east, the completing vāyu in the south, the metabolic (Skt. *samāna*, Tib. *me mnyam*) vāyu[61] in the west, and the moving vāyu in the north. These are the five vāyus of affliction and pristine consciousness. There are major and minor movements in the cakras of the nāḍīs that split off from the five secondary vāyus.

In some tantras, the upward-moving (Skt. *udāna*, Tib. *gyen rgyu*) vāyu, the downward-voiding (Skt. *apāna*, Tib. *thur sel*) vāyu, and the accompanying (Skt. *samāna*, Tib. *mnyam gnas*) vāyu are the great movements. The 21,600 movements of vāyu in a twenty-four-hour period are explained to be the minor movements. The upward-moving vāyu exists in the upper part of the body and performs the activity of inhalation and exhalation. The downward-voiding vāyu exists in the lower part of the body and performs the function of eliminating wastes, and so on.

60. The *avadhūti* nāḍī is the central nāḍī mentioned above. *Avadhūti* is translated into Tibetan as *kun 'dar ma*, literally, "to shake off everything."

61. The *samāna* vāyu appears as *mnyam gnas* in the new translation tantras and as *me mnyam* in old translation tantras as well as the system of Tibetan medicine.

The accompanying vāyu exists in the middle of the body and performs the activity of separating the pure and impure parts of food.[62]

Among the five vāyus that perform actions, the lifting vāyu generates the power of flesh and bone, performing the function of moving, sitting, stretching, and contracting. The generative vāyu exists in the spot between the brows and generates the strength of blood and lymph. The metabolic vāyu exists in the stomach and digests food. The vāyu that separates the pure and the impure at the two lower doors separates food and drink and performs the function of excreting feces and urine. Since the function-performing vāyus, which are inseparable from vidyā in the heart center, exist in the form of radiance, they cause concepts to arise as subject and object.

With respect to the bodhicitta element existing in those nāḍīs, the lunar bodhicitta flows through the *rasanā* from the inverted syllable *haṃ*, generating all tissues of the body. Specifically, it generates the brain, marrow, fat, and bone. The solar bodhicitta that flows from *a* through the *lalanā* generates flesh, blood, lymph, skin, hair, and body hairs. The purest of the pure essence—the pure essence that pervades everywhere [in the body]—arises and exists as the bindu of luminosity. The flow through the *rasanā* and *lalanā* is reversed in women. The red syllable *a* in the bliss-sustaining cakra is upright. The white *haṃ* in the *mahāsukha* cakra is inverted, existing as it is seen in the three nāḍīs. Specifically, the nāḍī of the supreme, unchanging luminosity, which is connected to the support of the great pure essence in the center of the body, exists in the center of the central nāḍī and pierces the two eyes.

During the seventh week, the phase of Viṣṇu resembling a tortoise, the body is the size of the mother's fist and extended thumb (*'khyid*). {388}

62. This vāyu is part of the tripartite system of metabolism detailed in Ayurveda and Tibetan medicine. Briefly, there is a *kapha* or *bad kan* (inaccurately translated in English as "phlegm"), called the *kledaka kapha* in Sanskrit or *bad kan myag byed* in Tibetan, which is the macerating function in the stomach. The second part of digestion (Skt. *pacaka pitta,* Tib. *mkhris pa 'ju byed*) refers to bile from the pancreas and gall bladder, which has the function of melting the macerated bolus that enters the small intestine. The metabolic vāyu (Tib. *rlung me mnyam*) then conducts the nutriment from the bolus into the small capillaries of the intestines and sends the waste into the colon through peristalsis.

During the eighth week, when the size of the body is the length between the mother's outstretched thumb and her pinky (*mtho*), until the thirty-sixth week, the body continues to grow, and then there is birth. At that time, the body is nine months and ten days old. After completing the ten stages, the nirmāṇakāya and placental dharma robe arrive with the sound of *ahaṃ* ("I am").

This is the formation of the body.

1.4 The Locations of Mind and Pristine Consciousness

There are two topics in the locations of mind and pristine consciousness. First is the location of pristine consciousness. When the body is formed in that way, pristine consciousness is also supported on the pure essence (*dwangs ma*),[63] which is the size of a mustard seed, inside the nāḍī of luminosity of the heart center. Pristine consciousness is a radiant light, which exists like a shiny wick or an ignited lamp, pervading the places of the four or five cakras. The radiance of the light one sees as an outer entity is located in the nāḍī, which is like a white silk thread, piercing the two eyes. Further, since the luminosity of the heart center—the transcendent state of the inseparable kāyas and pristine consciousnesses—exists in oneself, it has always pervaded all migrating beings. The *Śrī Māladevi Sūtra* states:

> The *sugatagarbha* pervades all migrating beings.[64]

The *Hevajra Tantra* states:

63. *Dwangs ma* (Skt. *rasa*) in this context refers to what is termed in the Great Perfection tradition the *rgyu'i thig le*, the material or causal bindu, which is formed at conception from the union of the father's and mother's reproductive tissue and the consciousness seeking rebirth. In the so-called "new translation" tantras, this bindu is generally referred to as the *mi shigs pa'i thig le*, or *anāhata bindu*.

64. Longchenpa identifies this passage as a citation from the *Śrī Māladevi Sūtra*; however, in the *Excellent Chariot*, p. 630, he identifies it as being from the *Moon Lamp Sūtra*, also known as the *Samādhirāja Sūtra*. The actual source of the line is Ratnākaraśānti's *Compendium of Sūtras*, 256b, where this line is added to a verse drawn from the *Samādhirāja Sūtra*, 32b–33a, which predicts that all sentient beings will attain buddhahood.

> Great gnosis abides in the body.[65]

The *Song of the Treasury of Couplets* states:

> That existence of gnosis[66] in the body will not be realized by [studying] all the treatises of paṇḍitas.

The *Tathāgatagarbha Sūtra* states:

> Within the bodies of all sentient beings, the *tathāgatagarbha* dwells immovably, just as it is originally.[67]

How does pristine consciousness exist? The body is endowed with a core composed of an empty essence, a clear nature, and compassion's cognizance. The inseparable three kāyas exist as a maṇḍala of clusters of the five families within a sphere of five lights inside the middle of the heart center, like a lamp in a vase. The *Universal Tilaka* states:

> In the celestial mansion of the precious heart center,
> the kāya is tiny, the size of a sesame seed,
> existing as complete, within a sphere of five lights.[68]

The *Compendium of Tilakas Tantra* states:

> The mental activity of sentient beings, inside the middle of the heart center, has the nature of three features.[69]

The three features are essence, nature, and compassion, like the example of a peafowl egg. The round and pure shape is the empty essence, the

65. *Hevajra Tantra*, 2a.

66. Here the original text has Skt. *buddha*, Tib. *sangs rgyas*.

67. This passage appears to be a paraphrase of the *Tathāgatagarbha Sūtra*, 24b, which runs as follows in translation, "The tathāgata dharmatā is immovable inside of those who are afflicted by all the afflictions."

68. Unattested.

69. CT, p. 240.

dharmakāya. The pattern appearing as the five lights is the clear nature, {390} the saṃbhogakāya. The core—vidyā—arises as the unceasing radiance of compassion, illustrating the nirmāṇakāya. The *Blazing Body of the Charnel Ground Tantra* states:

> Essence, nature, and compassion
> resemble the example of a peafowl egg.
> The transparent, round shape[70] is the dharmakāya;
> the rippled albumen[71] is the five lights, the saṃbhogakāya;
> and the pea chicks are the nirmāṇakāya.
> Thus, the illustration[72] is explained as the example.[73]

Further, the radiance of the five peaceful families of the heart center arises as the five wrathful families in the crown. The nāḍī that connects the heart center to the eyes, appearing as the crystal tube, is described in the *Pellucid Tilaka of Pristine Consciousness*:

> The king of nāḍīs, the crystal tube,
> exists piercing the sun and the moon.[74]

The light arising from that is the radiance of pristine consciousness emerging from the pathway of the nāḍī. The *Universal Tilaka* states:

> Connecting the precious [heart center] to the ocean,
> the smooth, white, hollow, empty nāḍī
> is not filled with bindu or blood.
> It is explained to be the path of pristine consciousness
> in which great pristine consciousness always moves.[75]

Also, when that is divided into five lamps, the heart center is the

70. Longchenpa gives /*dbyibs zlum dwangs pa*/ for CGT, /*dbyibs su grub pa*/. I have retained Longchenpa's reading here. In UM, he follows CGT.

71. Longchenpa here reads *chu ris* for CGT *chos nyid*.

72. Longchenpa gives *mtshon byed* for *sprul sku*.

73. CGT, p. 833.

74. UT, p. 165, incorrectly attributed to CT.

75. UT, p. 446.

lamp of the fleshy heart; the vidyā that exists there is the lamp of the supported basis; {391} the nāḍī that connects the heart center to the eyes is the lamp of the smooth white nāḍī; the eyeballs are the lamp of the watery far-reaching lasso, because they apprehend the reflection of luminosity; and the samādhi that arises from the unmoving luminosity is the lamp of the pristine consciousness of luminosity. Though taught as four in other cycles of the secret tilaka, here, since the practice is consistent with the unsurpassed cycle, five lamps occur. Since one meditates once one has recognized the pristine consciousness that abides in its own place, one is liberated on the original stage.

In brief, the essence of pristine consciousness is the mind essence—luminosity—the nature of the kāyas and the pristine consciousnesses. The location is the heart center, the path is the nāḍī, the doorway is the eyes, the field is the sky, and the function is original liberation.

Second, the essence of the mind is the potential (*rtsal*) that arises from the radiance of pristine consciousness, the all-basis that supports the impure concepts of subject and object, the group of eight, and the diverse traces.

The location is the nāḍī, which is the size of a stalk of wheat. It connects the lungs to the heart center, through which the karma vāyus move {392}, and bears the radiance of vidyā. When this arises in each sense gate, since it arises as analytical discernment (*rtog dpyod*), it is the lungs. The vāyu resembles a blind horse with legs. The radiance of vidyā is like a sighted, crippled man, who, once mounted [on a blind horse], can travel to various countries. The path is the connection between the heart center and lungs. From the lungs, the nāḍīs are connected to each sense gate. The doorways are the mouth and nose, the doorways of the movement of inhalation and exhalation. The doorways for arising in the field are the eyes, ears, nose, tongue, and body. The field is form, sound, scent, taste, and touch. The function is generating the causes and results of the deluded appearances of saṃsāra, because [the radiance of vidyā] arises as affliction. Though the entity that is the basis of arising of the mind is pristine consciousness, since the entity of the potential arises as subject and object, it is called "mind." Since pristine consciousness's own state is clear when the mind ceases, it is called "nonconceptual pristine consciousness." The import of this should be understood. The *Blazing Body of the Charnel Ground Tantra* states:

> The essence of the mind is pristine consciousness,
> which arises as the potential of subject and object.
> Since [pristine consciousness] uses the breath as the horse, it meets conditions . . .[76]
> The place is the abode of the windy house.
> The path is the throat, through which [the breath] moves.
> The door arises as the five[77] doors of desire. {393}
> The fault[78] is the arising of diverse concepts.[79]
> The function is creating the subject-object duality of saṃsāra.

Since pristine consciousness is encountered when the root of the mind is severed, that is the key point of the arising of empty clarity free from proliferation. When arising toward an object, mind is an aspect of the movement of that radiance. The knowing aspect is pristine consciousness. Since that knowing aspect and pristine consciousness are inseparable, they are neither the same nor different. The *Universal Tilaka* states:

> Mind and pristine consciousness
> are neither the same nor different.
> They are phenomena that are difficult to differentiate.
> The mind is the potential of pristine consciousness.
> The basis of the mind is pristine consciousness.
> Therefore, since mind and pristine consciousness
> are both the same and different,
> there is so-called "liberation" and "nonliberation."[80]

In brief, the location of the mind is the lungs. The doors are the nāḍīs,

76. These three lines and the final line are not attested to in CGT.

77. CGT reads *gsum*, following Longchenpa here.

78. Reading CGT *rkyon* for *rkyen*.

79. CGT, p. 829.

80. UT, p. 445.

the five sense organs, mouth, and nose. The path is the nāḍīs. The field is the sixfold group. The function is deluded vision. Since the radiance of vidyā in the heart center is stirred by the vāyu of pristine consciousness, it arises as luminosity. One's vidyā arises as the path of liberation in nirvāṇa.

Since the radiance of vidyā in the heart center is moved by the horse of the karma vāyu, its potential arises as concepts, {394} arising as the path of deluded saṃsāra because of ignorance.

The *Two Truths* states:

> The mind and mental factors that reify
> the three realms are concepts.[81]

For some Mādhyamikas it is necessary that the mind cease. The *Introduction to the Middle Way* states:

> The cessation of the mind is directly perceived by the kāya.[82]

Temporarily, the kāya of one's vidyā directly perceives the absence of conceptuality, and the path arises as luminosity. Ultimately, since the inseparable kāyas and pristine consciousnesses become the direct perception of the dharmakāya, the qualities of nirvāṇa are complete. Thus, it is very important to distinguish mind and pristine consciousness.

2. The Practice of the Path

There are two in the practice of the path: (1) the practice for this life, distinguishing mind and pristine consciousness; and (2) the stages of naturally perfected luminosity arising in the bardo.

81. *Verses on Distinguishing the Two Truths*, 3a.

82. *Introduction to the Middle Way*, 216b.

2.1 The Practice for This Life

There are two in the practice for this life: (1) practicing the intrinsic clarity of the mind without grasping, and (2) practicing pristine consciousness as naturally perfected luminosity.

2.1.1 Practicing the Intrinsic Clarity of the Mind

On the basis of the cognizance (*rig pa*) that arises for the objects of the sixfold group, look nakedly. {395} Since whatever is encountered is left completely as it is without grasping, once the discursiveness of the potential of vidyā is liberated in its own place, the experience of bliss, clarity, and nonconceptuality arise from within. When abiding without concepts because discursiveness is dropped, the radiance of vidyā is free from vāyu and moves to its own place as the luminosity of the heart center. Since the mind is liberated into pristine consciousness, it is called "the mind abides in its original place." After afflictions are liberated into pristine consciousness and one becomes familiar with that, it is called "luminosity is perfected in its original place." Many experiences of intense bliss, clarity, and nonconceptuality also arise.

2.1.2 Practicing Pristine Consciousness

Be seated cross-legged or with the knees up, either in a dark room or in daylight. The eyes should gaze about one cubit into the sky, and the mind should focus on that. Since the breath is very slow, it moves effortlessly. Having focused the intellect on the sky, tranquil and without thinking anything at all, the fundamental intellect (*gnyug ma'i yid*) relaxes in the state of the great perfection, and one meditates. If one is in a dark room, one will see smoke, mirages, rainbows, lightning, bindus, and forms of deities. If one is in daylight, rainbows, bindus, nets, tassels, {396} lotuses, forms, and so on, will arise. When those arise, since one does not move the eyes, one meditates on those without the mind wavering from its focus, and the self-originated pristine consciousness of emptiness and clarity arises from within, free from the extremes of proliferation. At that time limitless experiences of bliss, clarity, and non-conceptuality will arise, but one does not have clinging to joy. These appearances are the external appearances of the luminosity of the heart center. Whoever sees them is seeing the meaning of *sugatagarbha*, called "touching the pristine consciousness of luminosity." *Chanting the Names of Mañjuśrī* states:

> The vivid light of pristine consciousness,
> an illuminating great light, is the lamp of migrating beings.
> The lamp of pristine consciousness
> is a brilliant display, beautiful[83] to behold.[84]

Further, the basis appears in the sky from the heart center through the oceanic doorway of the eyes. The *Avataṃsaka Sūtra* states:

> Since the ocean is illuminated from the bottom,
> manifesting in the sky through the path,
> the maṇḍala of light is brilliant.[85]

Because of continual familiarity with that luminosity during the day and night, it increases more than before, and the forms of deities manifest as the maṇḍalas of the five families. {397} The *Guhyasamāja Tantra* states:

> [Meditate on a maṇḍala of buddhas that]
> abides in the center of the sky
> in a great cloud of light.
> The assembly of radiant buddhas
> is pervaded with radiant pristine consciousness.[86]

The *Compendium of Tilakas Tantra* states:

83. Here Longchenpa substitutes *lta na sdug* for *'od gsal ba*.

84. CNMa, 4b.

85. Unlocated.

86. *Guhyasamāja Tantra*, p. 770. The citation is present in an altered form. Tsham reads / *nam mkha' dbyings kyi dbus gnas pa/ sangs rgyas dkyil 'khor sgom pa ni/ 'od zer sprin gyi tshogs chen po/sangs rgyas 'bar ba'i 'od dang mnyam/'od zer sna lngas kun tu khyab/.*

> The diversity of one's radiance appears as the five families,
> arising from great, self-originated pristine consciousness.[87]

Such an appearance is a direct perception, the sublime key point of luminosity. The *Greatness of Samantabhadra Existing in Oneself Tantra* states:

> The self-appearance of consciousness is the key point of
> direct perception . . .[88]
> excellent pristine consciousness self-appears.[89]

After that, the increase of all appearances is exhausted, the material body is liberated into a mass of light, and the appearance of dharmatā—original purity—is like space. The *Universal Tilaka* states:

> The primal radiance of clear[90] dharmatā
> is like the early morning sky.[91]

At that time an inexpressible assembly arises in the eye: direct perception, the accomplishment of the four bases of magic power, the experience of appearances (clarity and emptiness), and mental experiences (bliss, clarity, and nonconceptuality). One should be diligent in these stages during the day and night. {398}

One may think that since luminosity appears in actuality in this aural lineage, it is not the secret cycle, however, though it is nominally designated "the secret cycle," this is defined as the aural lineage to prevent the decline of the cittatilaka tradition. The *Great Chronicle* states that this was named the unwritten aural tradition "in order that the tradition not decline."[37] The *Conch Writing* states:

87. CT, p. 245.

88. The tantra reads */rig pa rang snang mngon sum snang/*, but Longchenpa's reading is */shes pa rang snang mngon sum gnad/*. Since this citation occurs in the section where Longchenpa describes direct perception, it is likely that the reading of *snang* for *gnad* is incorrect.

89. *Greatness of Samantabhadra Existing in Oneself Tantra*, p. 203.

90. Longchenpa gives *gsal ba* for *dag pa*.

91. UT, p. 378. Here, reading *nam mkha'* for *zhogs pa*.

> This unsurpassed secret cycle
> is connected to the unwritten aural lineage.[92]

Therefore, [this aural lineage] is connected to the cittatilaka tradition. Since the unwritten aural lineage is abbreviated, it is designated the "secret cycle" because the major key points about the way the four visions arise, and so on, are absent. However, since this unwritten aural lineage explains pristine consciousness appearing to the eyes, it is superior to the written [aural lineage] because of the key points of the doors, and so on.[93]

2.2 The Stages of Naturally Perfected Luminosity Arising in the Bardo

In the stages of naturally perfected luminosity arising in the bardo, there are three topics: (1) the preliminaries, the way the elements gather; (2) the main subject, the way pristine consciousness arises; and (3) the conclusion, the way of progressing to the buddhafields.

2.2.1 The Way the Elements Gather

Those of medium diligence in this Dharma see appearances as filled with luminosity. However long they remain in equipoise,{399} that is the duration of the concentration of a calm mind. When those who recognize all self-appearances arising as the instruction of the bardo die, the earth vāyu dissolves into the water vāyu and the body becomes heavy because the ground of traces falls into earth. Since the water vāyu dissolves into the fire vāyu, the mouth and nose become dry. Since the fire vāyu dissolves into the air vāyu, warmth withdraws from the

92. *Conch Writing*, p. 269.

93. This appears to be a reference to a series of texts in the *Compendium of Tilakas* corpus that occur in the BGB and Tsham, in the same order, indicating this collection was cohesive by the twelfth century. One of these texts, *Child of the Compendium of Tilakas*, is explicitly authored by Chetsun Sengé Wangchuk. It is probable that the entire series of these texts was set down in writing by Chetsun Sengé Wangchuk.

extremities. Since the air vāyu dissolves into the nonconceptual space vāyu, consciousness becomes unclear. At that time the vāyu and mind in the lungs are not separated, and the radiance of vidyā dissolves into the heart center. All the remaining vāyu, which is like a blind horse, leaves the mouth and nostrils through the throat. When it cannot return, it is called "mind and pristine consciousness turn away from each other," and there is death. Further, since the so-called "mind" in the part of the radiance of vidyā carried by the vāyu is absent, it is the time when the entity of vidyā abides in the heart center. At that time the blood gathers into its pure part. When that gathers into the heart center, vidyā abides like a lamp in the center of the nāḍī petals of the heart center. When [the heart center] is struck by three drops [of blood], [vidyā] is expelled through the condition of terror and confusion.

2.2.2 The Way Pristine Consciousness Arises

There are three topics in the way pristine consciousness arises: {400} (1) understanding the key point of sound, light, and rays in the appearance of luminous pristine consciousness; (2) recognizing the maṇḍala of naturally perfected clusters as a self-appearance; (3) and seizing the ground of original liberation in the sheath of the precious secret.

2.2.2.1 The Key Point of Sound, Light, and Rays

When the pristine consciousness of vidyā emerges from the crystal tube into the watery lamp—the nāḍī pathway that connects the heart center with the eyes—the five lights, called "the tether of Vajrasattva," arise like a twisted cord from the right and left eyes. Since one abides in nonconceptual equipoise after focusing one's consciousness on that, those of best familiarity will be liberated in pellucidity above (*yar gyi zang thal*). If one is not liberated, then luminosity arises from that.

Then, though the time [the bardo of dharmatā] does not change, the appearances change, and there are no appearances of earth, stones, mountains, or cliffs. Everywhere one looks is pervaded by the brilliant appearance of the five lights. The intrinsic sound of dharmatā roars like one thousand thunderclaps. The lights shimmer like a mirage on the plains in the spring. Within the lights are rays that resemble a shower of weapons. The terrifying appearance of the wrathful ones arises, filling space. {401} Since one rests in the state of recognizing those appearances as one's own appearances, like one's face in the mirror, one attains buddhahood in the wrathful kāyas. If one does not recognize those kāyas, one will be terrified by the sound, panicked by the light, frightened by the rays, and faint because of the kāyas.

2.2.2.2 Recognizing the Maṇḍala of Naturally Perfected Clusters

After that, the radiance of the five pristine consciousnesses arises as the five lights, and the peaceful deities gradually arise. The *Large Compendium of Tilakas Tantra* states:

> Nonabiding pristine consciousness is the dharmakāya,
> bearing the characteristics of the five pristine consciousnesses.
> Self-originated pristine consciousness is the five elements,
> arising as the dimension of pure dharmatā.
> The bindus of five colors of light,
> manifesting as five colors—blue, and so on—
> are understood to be the essence of the buddhas of the five families,
> and the five kāyas [are understood to be] the perfect embodiment of pristine consciousness.
> Forty-two [kāyas] manifest as light.
> Each one dwells in the radiance of pristine consciousness,
> clear, brilliant, beautiful, and radiating rays of light.
> The celestial mansion of the five pristine consciousnesses
> has the nature of being pervaded with clarity, warmth, coolness,
> vastness, and lightness,
> a blazing mass of pristine consciousness that is the source of all.

The three seats,[94] which are not generated, are complete in the basis,
produce emanations through the three unions, {402}
and remove the darkness of the ignorance of migrating beings.[95]

At that time, having recognized self-appearances, since one rests in equipoise in that state, one is liberated in three moments. From the saṃbhogakāya state of one's mind, once the emanations of the six munis split off into the ten directions from the womb of the mother, the benefit of sentient beings is performed because of the union of the pristine consciousness of the three seats of body, speech, and mind. [*Chanting the Names of Mañjuśrī*] states:

Various emanations depart into the ten directions,
performing benefit in conformity with migrating beings.[96]

When the manner in which the five families arise is extensively analyzed, first, when blue is seen, through knowing this as a self-appearance in a single instant of equipoise, [one is liberated into the pristine consciousness of the dharmadhātu,] and there is the appearance of the maṇḍala cluster of Vairocana. Garab Dorjé's *Golden Rosary* states:

Abiding in the center and bearing the characteristics
of white, yellow, red, and green,
also, each [father] appears in the heart center
as a group of four—
a vajra, jewel, lotus, and crossed-vajra.
Also, the mothers are like the shadow of the body.
The first maṇḍala cluster
is a complete form in the seat of the basis.[97] {403}

94. The "three seats" refers to the five buddha family couples, corresponding to the five aggregates and the five elements; the male and female bodhisattvas, corresponding to the sense organs and sense objects; and the ten wrathful deities, corresponding to the ten joints of the body.

95. This citation is incorrectly attributed to the UT. It appears in the LCT, pp. 207–8.

96. CNMa, 8a.

97. Unavailable.

Second, when the white light appears and it is understood as one's own light, one is liberated into the mirror-like pristine consciousness and manifests as the maṇḍala of Akṣobhya. The latter text states:

> Vajrākṣobhya dwells in the middle,
> surrounded by Kṣitigarbha, Lāsya,
> Maitreya, and Dhupe,
> the second maṇḍala cluster.

Third, when one recognizes the yellow light, since it is understood as the pristine consciousness of uniformity, one is liberated as Ratnasambhava:

> Ratnasambhava dwells in the middle,
> surrounded by Akāśagarbha, Māle,
> Samantabhadra, and Puṣpe,
> the third maṇḍala cluster.

Fourth, when one recognizes the red light, since it arises as the individually discerning pristine consciousness, one is liberated as Amitābha:

> Amitābha dwells in the middle,
> surrounded by Avalokiteśvara, Girti,
> Mañjughoṣa, and Dvipa,
> the fourth maṇḍala cluster. {404}

Fifth, when one recognizes the green light, since it arises as the successful activity pristine consciousness, one is liberated as Amoghasiddhi:

> Amoghasiddhi dwells in the middle,
> surrounded by Vajrapāṇi, Nṛti,
> Nīvaraṇaviṣkambhī, and Ghande,
> the fifth maṇḍala cluster.

2.2.2.3 *The Sheath of the Precious Secret*

The sheath of the precious secret is the sheath of precious natural perfection, resembling the circuit of the sun, moon, and planets. Above is the appearance of the dharmakāya, the originally pure basis for the arising of the maṇḍala clusters, like the sky. In front is the saṃbhogakāya, like a rainbow, and below are various emanations of the six munis appearing in the six realms, performing benefit through teaching and arising in a single instant of self-recognition of the naturally perfected appearances. The four door guardians and the six munis appear to emanate and gather from maṇḍala clusters:

> Because of manifesting similarly,
> they arose from that [maṇḍala cluster]
> with form, color, and hand implements resembling the principal.
> The six munis engage in the benefit of beings,
> the four immeasurables tame them through the four door guardians,
> and the four female door guardians liberate them from the four extremes. {405}
> Since the dhātu and pristine consciousness are inseparable,
> those appear as Samantabhadra and Samantabhadrī.
> The mass of concepts is the qualities appearing as the five kāyas.

At that time, since the dharmakāya is the inseparable dhātu and pristine consciousness, one's light is blue, and the Samantabhadra couple are nondual in the appearance of original purity. In front, the maṇḍala clusters of the five families are Akaniṣṭha Ghanavyūha, the maṇḍala of the vajradhātu blazing as lights and rays. Below, when the inconceivable emanated forms of the six munis are in the places of the six migrations, after the three bodies are liberated, the three eyes dissolve, the six higher perceptions (Tib. *mngon shes*, Skt. *abhijñā*) arise, and one reaches the original basis.

The six higher perceptions occur when one is liberated through self-recognition. At that time, above, the higher perception of the eye sees the appearance of original purity, the basis of liberating the buddhafield of the dharmakāya beyond mind; in front, it sees the appearance of the Akaniṣṭha vajradhātu buddhafield of the saṃbhoga-kāya; and below, it sees the appearance of the six migrations to be tamed by the nirmāṇakāyas.

Above, the higher perception of the ear hears the great unsayable, unthinkable, and indescribable, because the speech of the dharmakāya dwells one-pointedly in pristine consciousness. {406} In front, the unchanging, pure, and clear speech of the saṃbhogakāya is heard. Below, the speech of the nirmāṇakāya with sixty tones is [rendered] in the language of each of the six realms. The first two kinds of speech are known as the inexpressible meaning. The third kind of speech is heard with the ears without grasping.

Above, the higher perception of the mind is knowing the transcendent state of the dharmakāya, inseparable wisdom and pristine consciousness. In front, the transcendent state of the saṃbhogakāya is known. Below, the transcendent state of the nirmāṇakāya is knowing how things are and what things are.

Above, the higher perception of place is the place the dharmakāya remains, the dharmadhātu free from proliferation. In front, it is the unchanging luminosity in which the saṃbhogakāya remains. Below, it sees the great field to tame, the self-appearance in which the nirmāṇakāya remains. The higher perception of karma is knowing all the results of natural karma. The higher perception of the base of magic power is knowing that emanations such as the six munis will tame those to be tamed. {407} Their functions are that the eyes distinguish, the ears hear, and the mind knows, causing awakening into original body, speech, and mind. [The function of the higher perception] of place is the buddhafields and engaging in beneficial activities for sentient beings. [The function of the higher perception] of karma is not entering into saṃsāra in the future, because all of one's delusions and traces are purified. Since compassion purifies the karma of sentient beings, they are tamed and led. [The function of the higher perception] of the base of magic power is to empty saṃsāra with great waves of benefiting others.

As such, these six higher perceptions actualize in totality all qualities of the buddhas.

The three bodies are the dissolution of the present body of flesh and blood into the pristine consciousness body in the bardo, which is liberated into the body of the precious dharmakāya.

The three eyes are the dissolution in the bardo of the present wisdom eye into the eye of dharmatā. Since the latter dissolves into the eye of precious pristine consciousness, there is original liberation.

As such, when the luminosity of the bardo arises as the luminosity of self-appearances, in the first moment, they are recognized and determined to be a self-appearance. In the second moment, since one is in equipoise based upon that determination, {408} one dwells in concentration. In the third moment, there is self-liberation and full awakening into the kāyas and pristine consciousnesses. In the fourth moment, the emanations benefit sentient beings. In the fifth moment, one abides without moving in the original state called "the transcendent state of luminous pristine consciousness." The fifth moment is also asserted to be the moment of completed activities.

2.2.3 The Conclusion, the Way of Progressing to the Buddhafields That Appear

The way of progressing to the buddhafields that appear: The person of average caliber in this Dharma has little diligence and becomes tired from just a little practice. Lacking time to practice, they have seen just a fraction of the appearance of luminosity, yet they have confidence in the instruction. They have no flaws in their samaya, yet despite this, when the luminosity of the bardo of dharmatā arises, they do not recognize it. Following this, through the blessing of the instruction, as soon as the naturally perfected bardo subsides, in a single instant they are born in any of these buddhafields: in the east, Abhirati; in the south, Replete with Gems; in the west, Sukhāvatī; in the north, Karmaprasiddhi; and in the center, Akaniṣṭha Ghanavyūha. At that time, they attain buddhahood. Some say that they are born in those buddhafields in the bardo of becoming in the amount of time of the duration of a dream.

Further, for those of very inferior caliber, even though they have seen luminosity, they do not practice, and at the time of death they do not remember the instructions. After the bardo of dharmatā subsides, the bardo of rebirth arises. When they recognize they are deceased, the best think of the instruction of luminosity and the buddhafields of the five families, and they are reborn there. Those of middling caliber engage in the illusory creation and completion stages. Those of average caliber go for refuge to the three jewels and are born with freedoms and endowments in Jambudvīpa or in the place of the devas in Tuṣita, and so on. After they meet Vajrayāna in this way, it is said they will be liberated. Thus, it is important to practice.

3. *The Way of the Liberation of the Result*

To explain the way of the liberation of the result, the best are liberated in this life, the middling are liberated in the bardo, and the average are liberated in another birth. The appearances of luminosity, or the kāyas and pristine consciousnesses, are exteriorized clarities. Because those dissolve into the state of original dharmatā, since the interiorized clarity—omniscience—exists as the three kāyas endowed with five pristine consciousnesses, even though the kāyas of liberation and the buddhafields do not appear externally, are not evident, and therefore do not manifest, {410} since there is no inner change, they always exist as the sole omnipresence. *Chanting the Names of Mañjuśrī* states:

> There is nirvāṇa, nirvāṇa,
> [those] close to excellent nirvāṇa,
> and the one who brings happiness and suffering to an end.
> Liberated and freed, the body of complete liberation
> is not evident, not apparent, does not [need] to be clarified,
> and does not change yet pervades everywhere.[98]

98. CNMa, 5b. This passage was translated based on Vimalamitra's *Lamp*, 23b–24a. According to Vimalamitra, the first nirvāṇa refers to *śrāvakas*, the second to *pratyekabuddhas*, and the third to *bodhisattvas*. "The one who brings happiness and suffering to an end" refers to *samyaksaṃbuddhas*.

The *Guhyagarbha Tantra* states:

> Not seen even by the Buddha,
> nonabiding, self-originated pristine consciousness appears.[99]

At that time there is (1) the meeting of the five elements with the mother, (2) the completion of the qualities of the five vāyus, (3) the dissolution of pristine consciousness into the dhātu, (4) the gathering of wisdom in space, and (5) vidyā taking its own place.

First, the coarse elements—earth, water, fire, air, and space—are the five that include the impure universe and beings. The five pure elements dissolve into luminosity. The five lights are the dhātu abiding as unchanging interiorized clarity. Air is Samayatārā, arising from the aspect of naturally perfected emanations, which emerge from the dhātu. Earth is Buddhalocanā, because hardness arises from the aspect of changelessness. Water is Māmakī, arising from the pristine consciousness and the dhātu merging inseparably without being differentiated {411} into something that gathers or separates. Fire is Pāṇḍaravāsinī, arising from the aspect of ripening those to be tamed through the heat of pristine consciousness. These are designated the samaya goddesses. Space is Dhatviśvarī, arising from the dhātu emptied of the basis of deluded vision and space-like original purity arising as pristine consciousness. As such, that is the time the five elements dissolve into inseparable, original luminosity.

The completion of the qualities of the five vāyus: Since the five females endowed with the power of the vāyu of pristine consciousness are in union with the principals of the five families of interiorized clarity as the nondual retinue, Keeper of Power (*shugs 'chang ma*) instantly moves into the state of the dharmakāya; Lifter (*'degs byed ma*) self-abides as the rūpakāya in the state of the dharmakāya without support and supported; and Stabilizer (*brtan ma*) is intrinsically clear without moving from the dharmakāya's transcendent state. In addition to the four pure secondary vāyus, Inseparable (*dbyer med ma*) always dwells in the peaceful dhātu, because the transcendent state of the kāyas and pris-

99. *Guhyagarbha Tantra*, 121a.

tine consciousnesses are inseparable in the space-like dharmatā that is neither one nor many. {412} At the time of impurity, those vāyus—the life-sustaining vāyu in the heart center and the four secondary vāyus—dissolve into the vāyu of pristine consciousness and are separated into different powers.

"Pristine consciousness dissolving into the dhātu" means that when the present analytical pristine consciousness arises as the radiance of vidyā, since it is the aspect of the nirmāṇakāya's omniscience of how things are and all there is, luminosity dissolves into the five pristine consciousnesses of the saṃbhogakāya—the mirror-like, uniformity, individually discerning, successful activity, and dharmadhātu pristine consciousnesses. These merge inseparably into the interiorized clarity of the original state and dissolve. At this time the three eyes and three bodies dissolve into one and become changeless in the sheath of the precious secret.

"Wisdom gathering into space" means that at that time, since there is no haze, the elements subside into the mother, and pristine consciousness dissolves into the dhātu. Though coarse exteriorized clarity does not exist, since the pristine consciousness of the inseparable three kāyas abides as interiorized clarity, the radiance of omniscient wisdom is intrinsically clear without ceasing. There are no concepts in clarity. At that time, since the essence is originally pure, {413} the saṃbhogakāya is adorned with major and minor marks in the state of the intrinsically clear pristine consciousness of the dharmakaya, free of proliferation. Since there are no concepts in the intrinsic clarity of the buddhafield of the youthful vase body, there is no thought of dualistic appearances. Since there is no body of traces, there is no movement of breath. Because of that key point, there are no concepts and there is existence, yet there is no self. At that time "existence" means that though there is vidyā—self-originated pristine consciousness—there is no mind that apprehends "I" and "mine." "Individuated but no gap is opened" means that at that time the appearance of the saṃbhogakāya arises without ceasing from the dimension of the dharmakāya, since no gap is opened by changing concepts, it always exists as naturally perfected. That is called "emptiness is the core of pristine consciousness."

There are four topics in vidyā seizing its own place: At that time, (1) the unchanging dharmakāya is a vajra-like kāya; (2) since pristine consciousness is unceasing, its longevity is like a swastika; (3) uninterrupted samādhi resembles a river of amṛta; and (4) the transcendent state is neither clarified nor obscured, luminous like the sun and moon.

First, since the apparent aspect of the rūpakāya of the dharmakāya is essenceless, {414} or selfless, the dharmakāya seems to be unchanging. The saṃbhogakāya is also unchanging like a vajra. Second, in the space-like state of the pristine consciousness of the dharmakāya, the pristine consciousness of the saṃbhogakāya is like the sun and moon. Since the pristine consciousness of the nirmāṇakāya produces a wheel that continuously turns to benefit sentient beings, it is unceasing, shining like light rays. Third, because of always abiding in the samādhi of unmoving dharmatā, and so on, there is no break in the transcendent state, like the bed of a river. Fourth, the knowing aspect of the transcendent state of the pristine consciousness of interiorized clarity abides in the transcendent state of luminosity, like the absence of obscuration in the orbs of the sun and moon. As it is neither clear sometimes nor obscured at other times, at all times it is clear without interruption, totally perfect.

These have four aspects: since within (1) the dharmakāya, a dimension like space, (2) the saṃbhogakāya, the great, naturally perfected interiorized clarity, always abides like the planets and stars, and (3) the nirmāṇakāya, like the moon reflected in the water, timelessly appears to tame whomever is to be tamed in the world to be tamed, {415} the activity of (4) pristine consciousness is vast, effortless, and uninterrupted for as long as space exists.

These principles have been slightly elaborated upon with reliable citations and set out briefly in accordance with what occurs in the most secret, unsurpassed tantras. Though it could be explained according to the vehicle of characteristics, out of fear for the excessive length of the text, it has not been elaborated for fear of prolixity.

In brief, when the concept apprehending a self rose out of the basis—the state of original luminosity—there was delusion into saṃsāra because of not recognizing one's state. While enjoying the diversity of happiness and suffering, buddhahood itself exists within oneself. Since one practices according to the profound instructions introduced by the guru, and since one recognizes the appearance of luminosity arising from oneself in this life, in the bardo, or in the next life, after one is free from saṃsāra, one will accomplish the intention of effortlessly accomplishing the two benefits. Thus, it is necessary to be diligent in practice.

Even though freedom and endowments are attained by someone in this life, those are impermanent and unstable like a water bubble, {415} perishable phenomena without substance. Those intelligent ones who wish for freedom seek a profound Dharma and principally engage in this path of the essence of luminosity. In the present degenerate age when there are few virtuous mentors and profound instructions are quite rare, those who practice in accord with the Dharma and bring it to culmination are even more rare. Children, if you abandon thoughts of this life, distance yourself from worldly affairs, and diligently meditate on the profound key points in isolated places, you will attain awakening in this life.

Also, after I swiftly accomplish liberation and swiftly travel to the stage of original exhaustion, may I rejoice immeasurably in the slightest benefit for others. Through the merit of setting out these words, may all migrating beings effortlessly accomplish the dhātu of the original basis after reaching supreme awakening, a wish-fulfilling cloudbank of inseparable kāyas and pristine consciousnesses that abide without ever changing.

The *Self-Appearing Direct Perception of the Definitive Meaning, The Great Aural Lineage* from the supreme secret tilaka, composed by Longchenpa, the yogi of the supreme vehicle, is complete.

Glorious protectress of mantra Zhanpa Sogdrup, Planetary King, and Dorjé Legpa, protect this! Samaya. Sealed, sealed, sealed. Virtue, virtue, virtue.

The Great Guide for the Path of the Supreme Secret

Oṃ āḥ hūṃ

> Homage to the feet of the sublime guru.
> The consolidated meaning of the profound key points
> of introduction, the stages of instruction
> from the unwritten secret tilaka, is written here for later generations.

From among the three topics, there are seven sections in the preliminary practices.

1. The Preliminary Practices

1.1 Guru Yoga

In the state of the universe appearing as the buddhafield of Samantabhadra, imagine the root guru and lineage gurus on one's crown and offer supplications.

1.2 The Yoga of Maṇḍala Offerings

Imagine the arranged heaps representing the four continents and Sumeru as a buddhafield and the enjoyments of the devas.

1.3 The Yoga of Vajrasattva

White Vajrasattva holds a vajra and a bell. {52} In his heart imagine the one-hundred-syllable mantra and recite it.

1.4 Employing the Impermanence of Longevity as the Path

Outwardly, there is the change of the four seasons. Inwardly, there is the change of the aggregates. Secretly, there is meditating on the perception of the bardo.

1.5 Weariness with Saṃsāra

Imagine the suffering of each of the six classes of migrating beings.

1.6 Cultivating Bodhicitta

Meditate by alternating giving all of one's happiness to the sentient beings of the infinite six realms and taking all of their suffering onto oneself. Meditate on great compassion.

1.7 Severing the Root of the Mind

There are three topics in severing the root of the apprehended objects and apprehending subject of the mind.

1.7.1 Outer Apprehended Objects

Outwardly, train in the absence of inherent existence of the five apprehended objects. In this way, all phenomena that appear as objects appear while not existing, like illusions and dreams. From the moment they appear, they lack a support. Meditate on the nature of nonabiding space.

Inwardly, to cut the root of the apprehending mind, since the entity of the mind that arises as the mass of conceptual affirmations and negations is investigated for its initial place of origin and its originator, where it remains and the agent that remains, where in the end it goes and the agent of going, {53} and its color and shape, the mind itself is realized to be like space, which demonstrates that saṃsāra and nirvāṇa are the same.

It is very important to train in these preliminary practices.

2. The Main Subject

There are two sections in the main topic, the introductions.

2.1 Introducing Original Purity as the Dharmakāya

For introducing original purity as the dharmakāya, which is the practice for this life, arrange a feast and *torma*s and offer supplications. Following the lineage, one should declare: "Look at the essence of one's present, naked, pellucid cognizance. It is clear and ungraspable, empty and selfless, cognizant yet unidentifiable. Since this is the dharmakāya, maintain one's own place in this state without distraction, fabrication, or adulteration!"

2.2 Introducing Natural Perfection as Luminosity

The introduction of natural perfection as luminosity for liberation in the bardo by showing what is to be seen [in the bardo] in the sun rays with a crystal is [introducing] the reality of the primordial original basis, the way Samantabhadra was liberated, the way ignorant sentient beings were deluded, the anatomy of the mind and pristine consciousness, the way the instructions are practiced, {54} and the introduction to the way of becoming liberated in the bardo.

Following the introductions, block the windows. There is the introduction of the trio of entering and abiding based on a human woman and arranging the wheel of symbols on the ground. By raising a crystal, also the three kāyas are introduced through the introduction of the example, meaning, and proof—the crystal, the sun, and the mask. Based on these, the crystal is the dharmakāya, the mask is the saṃbhogakāya, and the rays shining from the sun are the nirmāṇakāya.

In dependence on that, having made the introductions according to the lineage through the spectrum that results from holding a crystal up to a sunbeam, the path of the nāḍī that connects the heart center to the eyes is introduced; the time of the separation of mind and pristine consciousness is introduced; the appearance of the basis of the bardo is introduced; and the way sound, light, and rays arise is introduced. Finally, since the kāyas and pristine consciousnesses are inseparable in the sheath of the precious secret, while the interiorized clarity exists as the dharmakāya, exteriorized clarity acts to benefit others with the saṃbhogakāya and the nirmāṇakāya. These are the great guide for the path of the complete three aural lineages. {55}

3. The Subsequent Supporting Dharma

Having explained these either extensively or concisely, one should set the seal of the doctrine.

> As such, through the merit of composing the great guide of
> the path
> of the unwritten aural lineage,
> may all migrating beings enter this great vehicle
> and obtain the stage of the supreme victor, Samantabhadra.

The *Great Guide for the Path of the Supreme Secret* was completely set forth by Natsok Rangdrol, the yogi of the natural great perfection. Virtue, virtue, virtue.

Resting in Primordial Liberation

Homage to Śrī Samantabhadra.

Having paid homage to the state that never arose from the beginning, free from a basis or foundation,
the ordinary fundamental state that has always been just as it is,
since there is nothing to discard or establish, come or go,
listen to this brief explanation of the natural state!

All inner and outer phenomena of the universe, saṃsāra and nirvāṇa,
are primordially empty, naturally empty, and empty of inherent existence from the start.
Whatever way they appear, they are not established that way,
inherently free of the proliferations of existence and nonexistence, and permanence and annihilation.

Though appearing to the mind, [appearances] are not established as the mind, {56}
yet there is not an iota established apart from the mind.
Just as the appearances of one's dreams
appear while being nonexistent, [appearances] do not inherently exist at all.

While phenomena are not mind, nevertheless, there are no phenomena that arise apart from the mind—
not existent, not nonexistent, not true, also not false,

neither free nor not free from extremes, neither empty nor not empty—
whatever way one investigates, one cannot prove, "This is the way things are,"
because things do not exist in that way.

The nature of the sole dhātu that has been pure from the beginning
has been seen through many philosophical tenets by different minds.
Even though each asserts proofs of their own position,
caught in the net of conceptual analysis,
all simply designate names upon the authentic meaning.

In this way, all phenomena that appear to be objects
are not objects, lacking support, empty by nature in every way,
just like objects in a dream or a rainbow in the sky.
Whatever way they appear, in that way they are
vivid, clearly apparent nonexistents, like the eight examples of illusion.[100]
Whatever appears is inherently free of a basis or foundation.

Internally, the mind that apprehends a self is a mere imputation.
If sought, it cannot be found inside or outside. {57}
Vanishing without a trace, the searcher is intrinsically empty.
Without shape or color, uniform and limpid,
when looked for, the mind cannot be seen yet manifests when left just as it is.
Not illustrated by saying, "this is it," cognizance is beyond expression,
is not a partial entity, is not a position to identify,

100. Dreams, illusions, optical illusions, mirages, reflections of the moon in the water, echoes, fairy castles, and emanations.

without reference or identification such as empty or not
empty,
existent or not existent, is or is not, "what is it?" or "this is it."
Since there has never been a basis, path, or result,
why is there the proliferation of searching for a view,
meditation, conduct, or a result?

If one's mind eliminates the root of grasping,
without grasping and without a foundation, the limpid
dharmakāya
will be encountered as originally pure cognizance in which
thoughts and phenomena are exhausted.
More amazing than amazing, marvelous,
mind and its cognizance cause one to laugh, ha ha!

This thought that seems to exist but does not exist
is intrinsically empty because it depends on others.
Since it seeks emptiness, that seeker is lost in the middle.
Since the middle is searched for, because as before nothing is
found,
there is a single, nameless, traceless, limpid uniformity,
liberated without a "what?" a "why?" or a "this."

When relaxed about appearances, cognizance manifests
spontaneously.
Without support and free from a basis, appearances seem to
be pure. {58}
Everything is totally uniform, culminating in the
transcendent state of Samantabhadra.
One must laugh at something like that, ho ho!

Undefined appearances arise in a referenceless field.
Without grasping, cognizance is free and devoid of a position.
No matter how these arise, they are not established in that
way.
Everything is liberated without reference points.

Just like appearances in a dream,
grasping to duality is not established simultaneously;
subject and object are not perceived, having always been
empty, free of a foundation.
Mind and appearance devoid of a basis is the state of the
great perfection.

Having always been relaxed in repose, ordinary
consciousness
does not differentiate accepting and rejecting by clinging to
renunciation and antidotes—
rather, engaging whatever arises just as it is.
The binding fetters of clinging and grasping are saṃsāra.
Absence of grasping is the state of cognizance, nirvāṇa.
Saṃsāra and nirvāṇa are realized to be included in
cognizance without being accepted or rejected.
Affirmation and negation are realized to be included in the
fundamental state without being discarded or established.
The eight consciousnesses are understood to be included in
the mind without a basis or foundation.

Conceptual grasping vanishes, resembling the track of a bird
in the sky.
Arising and liberation are not separate, resembling water and
waves.
The apprehending subject and apprehended object are not a
duality, resembling objects and mind in a dream. {59}
Movement is insubstantial, resembling a breeze in the sky.
Vanishing is traceless, resembling a cloud vanishing in the
sky.
Cognizance is a pristine void, resembling pure space.
The limpid state abides in itself, resembling a calm sea.
That which is unceasing self-arises, resembling a pure mirror.
Cognizance is empty and limpid, resembling a stainless
crystal ball.

Naturally perfected luminosity is intrinsically radiant,
resembling the five lights.
The play of compassion is exteriorized clarity, resembling
apparent objects.
Saṃsāra and nirvāṇa self-appear, resembling the appearances
of a dream.
Nothing moves away from the dhātu, resembling the universe
in the dimension of space.
Deluded vision self-purifies, resembling waking from a
dream.
The inner dhātu is pure, resembling the new moon.
Original purity is immaculate dharmakāya, resembling space.
One who has such understanding is a wise person.

It is the state, it is primordial, and it is great luminosity.
There is nothing to discard or keep, to imagine or remove, to
radiate or absorb—
everything is in great repose.
Rest without modification, hope, fear, fabrication, or
adulteration!
It is the state, it is primordial, and it is liberated as the great
perfection. {60}
Blissful, clear, nonconceptual, with no center or border,
a relaxation devoid of effort arises from within.
Without hope and fear, the dharmakāya is effortlessly
accomplished.
Naked cognizance is peaceful and limpid,
the meaning that is beyond mind, mental factors, and
thoughts.
The realization of everything arrives at the original state of
exhaustion.

Astonishing! In the vast, great dimension of dharmatā,
the space of the nature without fabrication or adulteration—
bodhicitta in which nothing is discarded or established,
comes or goes—

rises the sun and moon free of thought, expression, and proliferation,
spreading light of bliss, clarity, and nonconceptuality,
self-originated pristine consciousness abiding just as it is.

In the unruffled, clear, and calm ocean
arise clear appearances, the reflections of the unimpeded five doors.
Rest in the state that is undisturbed by waves.
Observe reality, the essence without bottom or shore.

On a colossal, immovable mountain,
the transcendent state of nondual, fundamental equipoise arises,
liberated in that state of natural equipoise that has always been pure.
See the essence in which hope and fear, accepting and rejecting, are exhausted.

Attaining the result of the pure basis that has always been pure {61}
is the transcendent state of realizing reality.
That naturally resting cognizance, free from thoughts,
should rest effortlessly, free from falling into partiality!

If one remains in that state, everything is the dharmakāya.
Let it be with unceasing emptiness and clarity.
If there is a purpose, it becomes a cause of bondage.
Though it is selfless, free of proliferation, let it go.

If there is no identification of being and nonbeing, it is the original state.
Whichever way appearances and the mind arise, leave them as they are.
Bound by expectations and entanglements, one goes the wrong way.

Even undistracted samādhi should be released in the natural state.

If there is neither distraction nor nondistraction, it is the authentic meaning.
Though objects are engaged, relax and leave them just as one likes.
If one wishes for external purification, one is deluded.
Reference points are dispelled because nothing is established.
If there is no accepting or rejecting, hope or fear, it is the original dhātu.
Effort and accomplishment are dispelled through the dharmakāya abiding in its own state.

How wonderful! In the definitive meaning, dharmatā is the apex of the vajra essence.
There is no self and other, no saṃsāra and nirvāṇa.
Renunciation, antidotes, hope, fear, and effort are causes of bondage. {62}
How can dharmatā be realized by the vehicles of cause and result?
Just as the childish argue about whether or not space exists,
how can they reach the meaning from which nothing can be removed or be added to?
Will analysis that depends on provisional and definitive texts
ever see the reality of the essence that is free of proliferation?
Will valid cognitions of direct perception and inference
ever see the fundamental mind itself?
While unaffected by the taints of beginningless traces,
at present bound by the tethers of philosophical imputations,
one is surrounded by a fence of traces, never free from
the city of existence of the three realms and six classes of beings.
Since it is difficult to completely cut through the web of concepts,

how can people who have already cultivated this nature
enter the true meaning of dharmatā?

How sad! The foundation of saṃsāra is dualism.
The dualism of all conceptual ignorance increases exponentially.
The variety of happiness and suffering of saṃsāra is uninterrupted.
At what occasion is there liberation from the activity of completing activities?
Positive and negative are grasped in the mind through discriminations of "this" and "that,"
creating traces however they are grasped.
Positive and negative activities obscure the meaning of vidyā,{63}
like wrapping a gem with a soiled cloth.
The traces of virtuous actions and misdeeds that
divide the lower realms, and happiness and suffering, resemble dreams.
Even if one obtains a happy result in saṃsāra, which is compounded, inconstant, and impermanent,
it is unstable and meaningless.
Therefore, to reverse the traces that in this life
are the cause and source of suffering,
cultivate emptiness, peace, and selflessness.

Ho ho! The limpid consciousness of the view that does not grasp "this"
is free from fabrication and adulteration.
Free from the taint of duality,
sustain that state of reality of ultimate truth.
Free from bias toward movement or stillness, without thinking,
rest completely without distraction in the state of natural relaxation.
Hey, what can be easier than that?

Without searching, totally free from a searcher,
because there is no basis, foundation, or support, there is nothing to see when looking.
Release the state of natural relaxation in vast spaciousness.
The mind that does not identify cognizance or emptiness
is uniform and uninterrupted, resembling the pure sky.
Since it is free of hope and fear, deviations and obscurations are pure as they are. {64}
If that is understood, it is the yoga of the essence.
That is the view—emptiness and clarity free from proliferation.
That is the meditation—the state of empty intrinsic radiance.
That is the conduct—relaxing the group of six.
That is the result—the absence of both hope and fear.
Limpid cognizance encounters the stage of exhaustion.
If realized in this way, everything is free from a basis,
beyond the domain of the sense organs,
words and thoughts are exhausted,
and phenomena are just names, just words, and just designations.
Even though they are designated, they do not exist, just like the characteristic of space.
In self-originated pristine consciousness—pure, clear cognizance—
there is no view. Since there is nothing to see, there is no seer.
There is no meditation. Since there is nothing to see with meditation, there is no meditator.
There is no conduct. Since there is nothing to see with conduct, there is no one acting.
There is no result. Since there is nothing to accomplish as a result, there is no accomplisher.

In the mode of arising of self-appearing, unceasing cognizance, all exists.
When a facet is examined, everything exists—

there is appearance, there is emptiness, there is existence,
there is nonexistence,
there is truth, there is falsity, there is both, there is neither,
there is saṃsāra, there is nirvāṇa, there is uniform existence and peace,
there is creation, there is completion, there is method, there is wisdom, {65}
there is the nature, there is the primordial state, and there is the great perfection.
When the natural state is examined, nothing exists—
no existence, no truth, no appearance, no emptiness,
no truth, no falsity, no good and no bad, nothing to accept or reject,
no saṃsāra, no nirvāṇa, no creation stage, no completion stage, no union,
no method, no wisdom, no basis, no path, no result,
no self, no other, no duality, no gnosis,
no permanence and no annihilation, beyond speech, thought, and expression.

Having realized this, now I will sing a song!
In the yoga of the vast uniformity of everything,
since saṃsāra and nirvāṇa are liberated on the spot, the mind is easily found.
Since the root of hope and fear is severed, the basis is easily found.
Since one is free of doubt about being and nonbeing, the meaning is easily found.
Since one transcends thoughts of truth and falsity, oneself is easily found.
Since happiness and suffering arise as companions, joy is easily found.
Since the universe and beings arise as the guru, purity is easily found.

Since whatever appears arises as a text, words are easily found.
Since anything arises as an ornament, the nature is easily found.
Since everything encounters the stage of exhaustion, the primordial state is easily found.
Since all phenomena take their own seat, the result is easily found.
Everyone in the future should have this understanding!

Marvelous!
The sun of dharmatā arises in the vast dimension. {66}
Look at the tip of the victory banner that is never lowered.
The light of pristine consciousness that never sets shines
in the widespread, empty realms without a Sumeru.
Everything manifests as the transcendent state of the self-originated meaning
in the dimension in which there is no differentiation or exclusion, like an island of gold.
Look without wavering into the clear, undisturbed depths of
the waterless ocean of the limpid state!
Since the wish-fulfilling gem of qualities is naturally perfected,
it manifests naturally if one simply rests without wavering.
The light of the self-appearing sun and moon shines
on the unchanging, self-originated mountain.
The vast universe that is perfect without being constructed
is seen as the transcendent state of Samantabhadra permeated with bliss, permeated with himself.
The four continents are simultaneously visible from the peak of Sumeru.
Since the vast dimension of illuminated space is a great space,
everything is brought into the transcendent state of original purity.
This is the awakening of the original dharmakāya.

As such, may all migrating beings attain original
buddhahood
through Longchenpa's explanation
of the pinnacle of the Natural Great Perfection,
the meaning of the space-like, self-originated pristine
consciousness.

Resting in Primordial Liberation, composed by Natsok Rangdrol, the yogi of the king of vehicles, which plants the nail of the key points with a pinch of dharmatā, is complete. Virtue, virtue, virtue.

The Mind Mirror of the Aural Lineage

Homage to Śrī Samantabhadra.

> I shall write the *Mind Mirror* of the aural lineage of the tilaka series,
> the core of all scriptures, extracts, and intimate instructions,
> the refined essence of the outer, inner, and secret tilakas
> that is the Natural Great Perfection.

There are three in the explanation of the immaculate single eye of pristine consciousness: (1) the chronicle of the amazing lineage, (2) the way the instruction is illustrated through the introduction, and (3) the stages of setting the seal of the prized doctrine.

1. The Amazing Lineage

The Bhagavān Samantabhadra gave the explanation through the natural blessing of the transcendent state. Vajrasattva taught Garab Dorjé through well-arranged words. Garab Dorjé taught Ācārya Mañjuśrīmitra. Ācārya Mañjuśrīmitra taught Ācārya Śrī Siṃha. Ācārya Śrī Siṃha taught Mahācārya Vimalamitra.

For the lineage of esteemed personages, King Trisong Detsen gave the translators Ma Rinchen Chog (*rma rin chen mchog*), Kawa Paltsek (*ska ba dpal brtsegs*), and Cokro Lui Gyaltsen (*cog ro klu'i rgyal mtshan*) a large amount of gold powder and sent them to invite Mahācārya Vimalamitra. When Vimalamitra arrived, he taught many outer and inner dharmas. He examined who was a suitable recipient for this aural lineage.

He went to Hepori, observed Nyak Jñānakumara, and observed that he was an unsuitable recipient. Vimalamitra said to Nyang Tingzin Zangpo, "In general, gold is valued in Nepal to the south. In particular, the people of India value gold. After you have sold your entire estate, will you give your gold to me?"

Nyang thought, "Since Vimalamitra didn't want the king or Nyak, but instead wants me, it is necessary to make an offering to gather accumulations."

Since Vimalamitra knew Nyang's thoughts, he said, "I don't need gold. I was examining your suitability as a recipient, and you are a suitable recipient."

Then, at that time, he taught Nyang the aural lineage. Nyang taught this to Bé Lödro Wangchuk (*sbas blo gros dbang phyug*). Bé taught this to Dromtön Rinchen Bar (*'brom ston rin chen 'bar*). Dromtön taught this to Sthavira Dangma Lhungi Gyaltsen (*gnas brtan ldang ma lhun gyi rgyal mtshan*). Dangma taught this to Chetsun Sengé Wangchuk (*lce btsun seng ge dbang phyug*). Chetsun taught this to Guru Shangpa Repa (*gu ru shangs pa ras pa*). Shangpa Repa taught this to Lama Zabtön Chöbar (*bla ma zab ston chos 'bar*). Zabtön taught this to Tsari Dampa Gyerzhig (*tsā ri dam pa dgyer zhig*). Dampa Gyerzhig taught this to Nyentön Sherab Tsemo (*gnyen ston she rab rtse mo*). Nyentön taught this to the peerless tulku brothers. They taught this to Lama Namkha Dorjé (*bla ma nam mkha' rdo rje*). Namkha Dorjé taught this to Rigzin Kumarāja (*rig 'dzin ku ma rā ja*), who in turn taught it to the scholar Natsok Rangdrol (*sna tshogs rang grol*).[101]

2. *The Way the Instruction Is Illustrated through the Introduction*

There are four topics in the way the instruction is illustrated through the introduction: (1) the examination of the basis for the reality of the abiding basis; (2) the examination of delusion for the path, the way delusion

101. This is a name used by Longchenpa throughout the *Zabmo Yangtik*, along with "Drimé Özer" and "Longchen Rabjam."

is deluded; (3) the examination of the instructions for the three grades of calibers, the method of reversing the delusion to be reversed; and (4) the examination of the six bardos for the way the liberated result is liberated.

2.1 The Examination of the Basis

There are two topics: (1) the reality of the original basis, and (2) the basis of Samantabhadra's liberation. {70}

2.1.1 The Reality of the Original Basis

First, before saṃsāra and nirvāṇa were established at all, the self-originated pristine consciousness of vidyā existed possessing five features: its essence is empty; its nature is clear; its compassion is unceasing; its qualities are unchanging; and its activities are unimpeded, present as an undifferentiated, single, original dhātu.

2.1.2 Samantabhadra's Liberation

When the radiance of the clear nature arose externally from the state of the empty essence, since cognizant compassion recognized its own appearances as pristine consciousness, as the unimpeded activity of the appearance of the basis of qualities arising as the kāyas and pristine consciousnesses was liberated into the inner dhātu, the originally pure essence, there is buddhahood without ever moving away from the original basis. Further, since Samantabhadra knew the meaning of the basis at the start, he realized it to be the unchanging essence; since he knew the cause and condition in the middle, he realized the five lights of the appearance of the basis as intrinsic radiance; and in the end, since he knew that the self-arisen is self-liberated, he took his own ground as the intrinsic radiance of the liberation of the basis, arising as the original protector called "Bhagavān of Great Knowledge." {71}

2.2 The Examination of Delusion, the Path

Since that arising of the appearance of the basis from the basis was not recognized, conceptual grasping arose and wandering in saṃsāra ensued. Since the intrinsic radiance of the basis endowed with five features[102]—the five lights—was not recognized as intrinsic radiance, subject and object were discriminated by means of the apprehender and the apprehended, and the basis's own appearance formed as the deluded appearances of saṃsāra. Now, since the empty essence was not recognized, vidyā did not rise out of the basis. Since the clear nature was not recognized, there was delusion into the body and objects. Since unceasing compassion was not recognized, the mass of concepts[103] arose as the mind (*sems*). Since the changing qualities were not recognized, [the basis's] own potential arose as the appearance of faults. Since the activities were not understood as unimpeded, through cycling in saṃsāra's highs and lows, one experiences the dream-like deluded appearances of the bodies, locations, happinesses, and sufferings of the four kinds of birth.

2.3 The Way Delusion Is Reversed

Among the four ways of giving instruction that is to be understood to the persons of the three calibers, there are five dharmas for those of the highest caliber: confirming appearances as mind, {72} confirming the mind as empty, confirming appearance and emptiness as inseparable, confirming many as one taste, and confirming pristine consciousness as continuous.[104] For those of middling caliber, there is confirmation with five examples:[105] confirming appearances as mind with the example of sleep and dreams, confirming the mind as empty with the example

102. Essence, nature, compassion, qualities, and activities.

103. Reading *rtog* for *rtogs*.

104. The example and meaning are ascertained together.

105. Longchenpa here mentions five examples but gives only four.

of empty space,[106] confirming many are one taste with the example of water and ice, and confirming pristine consciousness is uninterrupted with the example of a flowing river.

When all phenomena of the universe and living beings are included within the necessities for a single person, all are included in the teaching of the Great Perfection. That teaching also includes view, meditation, conduct, and result. The view is empty cognizance. The meditation is the intrinsic clarity of the limpid state. The conduct is the self-liberation of attachment and aversion. The result is immaculate pellucidity. Those of middling caliber wear four ornaments: they wear the ornament of pristine consciousness on the empty view, the ornament of nongrasping on the intrinsic clarity of meditation, the ornament of a peaceful nature on self-liberated conduct, {73} and the ornament of naked cognizance[107] on the immaculately pellucid result.

Again, view, meditation, conduct, and method are included in the four necessities for a single person, and the result is implied. The view is unfabricated, the meditation is nonconceptual, the conduct is without clinging, and the method is nondistraction. To introduce these four, the unfabricated view is introduced as the fundamental consciousness (*gnyug ma'i shes pa*). The unfabricated meditation is introduced as ordinary consciousness (*tha mal gyi shes pa*). Conduct without clinging is introduced as relaxing the group of six. The undistracted method is introduced as continuous mindfulness.

Among the trio of people of highest, middling, and average caliber, there are none who are not included in the set of twenty-one.

The person of highest caliber (1) understands the way things are, (2) abides in the state, (3) is decisive, (4) benefits the mind, (5) maintains mindfulness, (6) does not give rise to concepts, and (7) has realization. There are three methods of equipoise: (1) resting like a cloud in the sky, (2) resting like a grindstone with the water cut off, and (3) resting like a person who has finished work.

For a person of middling caliber, (1) if they are unable to understand

106. The example of confirming the inseparability of appearance and emptiness is absent.

107. Reading *rig pa* for *rigs*.

the way things are, they should examine deviations and obscurations; {74} (2) if they cannot abide in the state, their consciousness falls under the power of conditions; (3) if they cannot be decisive, they chase after objects; (4) if their mind is not benefited, they are no different than regular people; (5) if they cannot maintain mindfulness, they are lost in the five poisons and the three poisons; (6) if nonconceptuality does not arise, they get lost in their own afflictions; and (7) if they have no realization, they create seeds of saṃsāra. Thus, there are seven examinations. There are three methods of guarding: (1) like guarding a wild horse, (2) like guarding the king's queen, and (3) like guarding a wish-fulfilling gem.

The person of average caliber should (1) investigate whether or not there is confidence in understanding the way things are; (2) for abiding in the state, investigate whether or not there is benefit or harm; (3) for being decisive, investigate whether or not one is lost to the five poisons; (4) for benefit to the mind, investigate whether or not the fundamental root has been cut; (5) for maintaining mindfulness, investigate whether or not there is liberation in its own place; (6) for the arising of nonconceptuality, investigate whether or not the clarity aspect has been exposed; (7) for realization, investigate whether or not there is a realizer.

There are three introductions: (1) both the pleasant and unpleasant objects of visual appearances, which lack inherent existence, are introduced, likened to {75} the moon reflected in the water; (2) both the pleasant and unpleasant sounds for the ear are introduced, likened to echoes in an empty valley; and (3) all the discursiveness of affirming and negating memories and concepts as mental objects is introduced, likened to a monkey in an empty house.

Thus, there are twenty-one factors and nine methods, totaling thirty, which explain the practices for people of the three calibers.

Within the necessities for a single person, the essence of the view is unchanging emptiness, the essence of meditation is not grasping intrinsic clarity, the essence of conduct is impartial self-arising, the essence of instruction is the uncorrupted way things are, and the essence of the result is immaculate purity.

Again, the four activities of view, meditation, conduct, and result are explained within the necessities for a single person. The activity of the view is to abandon the apprehended object and the apprehending subject, the activity of meditation is to abandon affliction, the activity of conduct is to abandon partiality and bias, and the activity of the result is to abandon hope and fear.

The instruction of the sublime guru is to give up mundane activities. If these activities are not given up, one is a regular person. If they are given up, one is a true person. The outer apprehended object and the inner apprehending subject are abandoned with the view of unchanging emptiness. If the apprehended object and apprehending subject are not abandoned, [yoga] is corrupt gossip. {76} If they are abandoned, yoga is correct. The afflictions—whose nature is the five poisons—are abandoned by the meditation that does not grasp intrinsic clarity. If afflictions are not abandoned, one is named "great meditator." If they are abandoned, one is a true bodhisattva. Partiality and bias for positive and negative, and accepting and rejecting, are abandoned with self-arising impartial conduct. If partiality and bias are not abandoned, conduct is superficial, but if abandoned, it is the true destruction of delusion. The immaculate result abandons the banks of hope and fear of the apprehended object and apprehending subject. If hope and fear are not abandoned, [the result] is a mental aspiration for a future time. If abandoned, it is true buddhahood.

The explanation of the four measurements: If there is neither an apprehended object nor an apprehending subject, view has been brought to its measure. If there is neither lethargy nor agitation, meditation has been brought to its measure. If grasping and attachments are pure like space, conduct has been brought to its measure. If there are no taints in the mind, experience has been brought to its measure. If saṃsāra and nirvāṇa are undifferentiated, the result has been brought to its measure.

The five examples: The example for the instruction of intrinsically radiant appearances is the simile of rain. The example for the cognizance of equipoise is the simile of gold. In post-equipoise, the example for abiding in the fundamental state is the simile of an infant. The example for abiding continuously in the three times is the simile of the river. {77} The example for transcending expression is the simile of space.

Again, within the necessities for a single person to fight saṃsāra and nirvāṇa, there are four armors to don, four straps to tighten, four weapons to wield, and four enemies to slay. Among the four armors, donning the armor of faith is patience for difficulty. Donning the armor of hearing is eliminating outer and inner doubts. Donning the armor of diligence is practicing the *sādhana*. Donning a low position is not holding a prestigious rank. Among the four straps, there is the strap of not fearing the two difficulties,[108] the strap of not doubting the instruction, the strap of not allowing experience to dissipate, and the strap of not grasping to one's continuum as real. Among the four weapons, wield the weapon of the view and slay the enemy, partiality and bias; wield the weapon of meditation and slay the enemy, lethargy and agitation; wield the weapon of conduct and slay the enemy, superficiality; and wield the weapon of the result and slay the enemy, hope and fear. Among the four enemies to slay, slay the outer enemy, the eight worldly dharmas; slay the inner enemy, the five poisons and the three poisons; slay the secret enemy, grasping to "I" and "mine"; {78} and slay the ultimate enemy, ignorance.

The yogi who practices that way attains buddhahood through the four seals: buddhahood in the manner of the lion sealed in a womb, buddhahood in the manner of a *garuḍa* sealed in an egg, buddhahood in the manner of a sun and moon amulet, and buddhahood in the manner of a yogi sealed in the body.

2.4 Liberating the Result

The examination of the six bardos—the way the result of liberation is liberated—has three topics: (1) the essence of the bardo, (2) the definition of the bardo, and (3) the divisions of the bardo.

108. Reading *dka'* for *bka'*.

2.4.1 *The Essence of the Bardo*

The essence of the bardo is that it is the interval (*bar do*) between the appearance of the basis stirring from the dhātu until all the positive and negative self-appearances are liberated into the dhatu. These bardos are (1) the appearances of pure nirvāṇa—luminous dharmatā—appearing as the kāyas and pristine consciousnesses; (2) the deluded appearances of impure saṃsāra, past and future lives as well as the bardo of dreams; and (3) the experiential appearances of the samādhi of the path and their projected potential, vidyā arising as outer and inner activity.

2.4.2 *The Definition of Bardo*

The definition of bardo: Since it is the phenomenon of the interval between vidyā abiding in its own place and taking its own place, it is called *bar*. Since it is the appearance of the basis, it is called *ma*. {79} Since it is the appearance of both saṃsāra and nirvāṇa in connection, it is called *do*.[109]

2.4.3 *The Division*

There are six divisions of the bardo: (1) the natural bardo, (2) the bardo of samādhi, (3) the bardo of dreams, (4) the bardo of death, (5) the bardo of dharmatā, and (6) the bardo of existence.

2.4.3.1 *The Natural Bardo*

The natural bardo is spending all of one's time enjoying the apparent objects of the six senses from birth until one is struck by an illness that is the condition for death. One eliminates doubts of hearing and reflecting on the dharmatā of vidyā, one practices the meaning like a swallow entering its nest, and everything is determined to be a self-appearance. The *Divine Heap of Jewels Tantra* states:

109. Literally, "between (*bar ma*) two (*do*)."

> Looking there, manifesting here,
> like one's reflection in the mirror.[110]

2.4.3.2 *The Bardo of Samādhi*

Since one remains in a clear, pristine, limpid, unceasing radiance in a state of empty, clear cognizance, practice like a rainbow arising in the sky. A mind series citation states:

> Clear, objectless, and undisturbed
> is explained to be the intention of pure yoga.[111]

2.4.3.3 *The Bardo of Dreams*

After one goes to sleep and while one has yet to awaken, the apprehension of the objects of the five doors withdraws inside, which is the period when everything arises as a single mental consciousness based on the all-basis consciousness. {80} In the practice here, as one is undistracted in recognizing the meaning of clarity and nonconceptuality, one continues in samādhi in that state when one goes to sleep, and the delusions of dreams cease, like the course of a river. The *Hevajra Tantra* states:

> Like a flowing[112] river
> and the bright flame of a lamp,

110. *Divine Heap of Jewels Tantra*, p. 470. This tantra is included in the outer and inner cycles in the *Gting skye* NGB. These two lines are from separate verses, the first following the second: */grol ba gzhan rkyen ma yin te// rang rkyen shes pa grol bar bstan// me long byad kyi dpe bzhin no// thig le ye shes khong nas shar// phar bltas pas na tshur la gsal// ye shes zang thal kho na yin*. "Liberation is not from external conditions; rather, liberation is explained to be knowing one's own condition, like a reflection in a mirror. Since the bindu arises from within pristine consciousness—while looking there, it manifests here—it is only pellucid pristine consciousness."

111. Unidentified.

112. Following the *Hevajra Tantra*, reading *rab bab* for *rang bab*.

since yoga is constant, day and night,
it is reasonable to engage only in this.[113]

2.4.3.4 *The Bardo of Death*

When the elements dissolve into four parts due to being caught by the condition of death, one's consciousness becomes confused, unstable, unfocused, and hazy. One must be one-pointedly focused on the meaning that one has meditated on previously and the instructions for the bardo, like threading the eye of a needle. A mind series citation states:

Recognize the reality of the bardo of death
with unwavering mindfulness,
like threading the eye of a needle.[114]

2.4.3.5 *The Bardo of Dharmatā*

Since space dissolves into luminosity, appearances of outer earth, stone, mountains, and cliffs cease, and appearances self-appear as the buddhafield of the five pristine consciousnesses. Inwardly, the delusions of mind and mental factors cease, and there is self-abiding in natural samādhi. {81} The whole universe self-arises as the buddhafield of kāyas and pristine consciousnesses. When it manifests as the maṇḍala of the saṃbhogakāya, there is confidence in self-appearance, and because one remembers the intimate instruction of the simile of crawling onto the mother's lap, after the appearance of the basis dissolves into the dhātu, there is buddhahood. *Chanting the Names of Mañjuśrī* states:

Differentiated by a single moment,
there is perfect buddhahood in a single moment.

113. *Hevajra Tantra*, p. 348. The passage given here is a variant of the canonical text. The two final lines here read, */nyin mtshan rtag tu rnal 'byor pas// 'di nyid 'ba' zhig spyad par rigs/*.

114. Unidentified.

At that time, since the five afflictions become as pure as the five pristine consciousnesses, there is no cause for birth in saṃsāra. Since the five lights dissolve into the pure dhātu, the basis of deluded objects self-reverses. Since one's vidyā is liberated into its original state, it is devoid of grasping a self. Since the three doors are liberated as the three kāyas, the source of the delusion of the three realms is exhausted. Since there are no apprehended outer objects, there is no place of arising. Since there is no inner apprehending mind, there is no sentient being who is an agent of arising. Since saṃsāra and nirvāṇa are liberated into the original basis, there is buddhahood in the dimension of the sole unique dharmakāya, reality. At that time, since there is buddhahood in the dimension of limpid pristine consciousness beyond the kāyas, {82} there is buddhahood in the dimension of pure omnipresent dharmakāya beyond objects; there is buddhahood in the ultimate dimension of mind, the transcendent state of buddhas beyond nonduality; there is buddhahood in the dimension of the five pristine consciousnesses, natural perfection beyond phenomena; and there is buddhahood in the dimension of omniscience of all aspects beyond the basis. Though that is omniscience at the time of the basis, since the result is pure because of being liberated through one's recognition, it is called "the pristine consciousness of omniscience of all aspects." Since it appears as the omniscience of inner clarity and the omniscience of all aspects of outer clarity, ultimately both are naturally perfected, present without changing from the original dhātu.

2.4.3.6 *The Bardo of Existence*

The bardo of existence is the interval between separating from the body of this life, once the bardo of dharmatā vanishes automatically since it was not recognized, until one appropriates the body of the next life. Like the body and appearances of a dream, consciousness at this time is seven times clearer. All sense organs are complete. One can travel without being impeded by anything other than the womb of a mother or Vajrāsana. One possesses miraculous action. {83} One can see everything outside, yet no one can see one other than those of the same class [other bardo beings] and those who possess the deva eye. Since one's consciousness is free from a support, one is naturally fearful and feels cold. Since one remains confused and hazy, one hurries to find a body. At that time, one should recall the instruction that is like repairing a broken pipe: Those of highest caliber understand the bardo to be false and are liberated without grasping. Those of middling caliber understand the bardo to be illusory and are liberated through natural creation and completion. Those of average caliber go for refuge to a buddha in a pure buddhafield, and through sincere aspiration they are born as the child of faithful parents in a body with freedoms and endowments, after which they will encounter the intimate instructions of profound points, the Dharma of their final existence, and during that lifetime or in the bardo attain complete buddhahood.

That is the examinations of the six bardos.

3. *Setting the Seal of the Prized Doctrine*

The stages of setting the seal of the prized doctrine: Apply oneself to practice in four sessions. Always remember the guru. Do not explain the secret intimate instructions to unsuitable recipients. Do not deprecate the cause and effect of karma. {84} Increase pure vision and devotion. In particular, since this Dharma is owned by the ḍākinīs, practice it in total secrecy. Since these are the root samayas, I ask you to please refrain from delusion of the three doors with respect to the guru and siblings and have devotion for them.

By setting down in writing the pinnacle of the most profound
vajra essence,
supreme among the essential intimate instructions of the
guru,
for the benefit of later generations,
may all migrating beings attain awakening.

Having been born deluded by grasping "I" and "mine,"
having meditated on the essential meaning of the self-
appearance known for oneself,

at this time of the saṃsāric ocean of birth and death,
may the nonabiding, imperceptible nirvāṇa be attained.

This approach that illuminates the darkened sky of my
[mind] and others' minds
through shining one thousand *light rays* of wisdom
in the space of the *immaculate* dharmadhātu
was well composed on the slopes of Gangri Thökar.

The *Mind Mirror of the Aural Lineage* was written in its entirety on the slopes of Gangri Thökar by Drimé Özer, the yogi of the supreme vehicle. Virtue, virtue, virtue. {85}

The Ultimate Mirror of the Aural Lineage

Homage to Śrī Samantabhadra.

I bow to the feet of the one who attained full awakening in
the original abode,
the original buddha who effortlessly accomplished the two
benefits,
inseparable from the kāyas and pristine consciousnesses;
to the gurus of the lineages of the vidyādharas; and to
esteemed persons.

For future generations I have clarified
this precious unwritten aural lineage,
the Dharma of the profound key points from the
unsurpassed, secret, supreme tilaka,
transmitted from one generation to another.

The doctrine of the Great Perfection is the supreme pinnacle
of all vehicles,
the sap of the trio of tantra, *āgama*, and *upadeśa*,
the refined essence of the outer, inner, and secret tilakas,
and the intention of all buddhas of the three times.

It is the ultimate conclusion of view, meditation, and conduct,
it is the key points of basis, path, and result,
it shows the three doors to be self-liberated,
it shows the three kāyas to naked sight,

> and it shows buddhahood to be held in one's hands,
> heard through a lineage one after another.

There are three topics in the *Ultimate Mirror of the Aural Lineage*: (1) the chronicle of the lineage's source for confidence, (2) the intimate instruction of how the instruction is bestowed, and (3) the instruction concerning the introduction for realization and liberation. {86}

1. The Chronicle of the Lineage

There are three topics in the chronicle of the lineage: (1) the transcendent state lineage of the victors, (2) the symbolic lineage of the *vidyādharas*, and (3) the aural lineage of esteemed persons. The *Major Universal Tilaka Tantra* states:

> There are three topics in the chronicle:
> Since they are not temporary persons,
> the lineage of the buddhas of the three times is explained.
> One can be confident in the teachings from the mouths of the buddhas.
> Since the retinue is definitive,
> the symbolic lineage of the *vidyādharas* is explained.
> One can be confident that the definitive meaning is taught,
> rather than the indirect, implicit meaning.
> Explain the aural lineage of the esteemed persons of the future.
> One can have confidence since the lineage is uninterrupted.

1.1 The Transcendent State Lineage of the Victors

Among the three topics in the transcendent state lineage of the victors, the first is the dharmakāya's teaching through blessing. From the specific place, the dharmadhātu, Clear Blissful Lotus City (*pad ma bde gsal gyi grong khyer*),[115] without high, low, center, or periphery and not established as any kind of entity, the mental agent (*yid byed pa po*) arose in the form of Samantabhadra himself with faces and hands and taught the essence of the doctrine, the five pristine consciousnesses, to the retinue that realized these as a self-appearance, the five families, at an undefined time through natural blessings. The *Compendium of Tilakas Tantra* states:

> In the past,
> in Clear Blissful Lotus City,
> I, the teacher, All-Knowing Lord of Dharma,
> as a nonconceptual blessing
> taught the heart of the doctrine, the five pristine
> consciousnesses,
> to the retinue that realized these as a self-appearance.[116]

And the *Secret Array of Vidyā Tantra* states:

> The time of the explanation through the blessing of the
> dharmakāya
> is the time when the vajra of realization self-appears.[117]

The saṃbhogakāya's teaching through intrinsic nature: The specific place is the buddhafield of Vajradhara with full characteristics, the dharmadhātu palace of Akaniṣṭha. The teacher is Vairocana and the retinue of four, such as Vajrasattva, and so on, and the four families. The time is when vidyā arises in the field. The teaching is the transcendent state of inseparable kāyas and pristine consciousnesses—in fact, [it is] essentially beyond words. The *Compendium of Tilakas Tantra* states:

> The Teacher, All-Knowing Pristine Consciousness,
> drew a maṇḍala of the ceaseless pristine consciousness
> that arises from the intrinsic radiance of clear dharmatā,

115. This name of the dharmadhātu is unique to the tilaka tantras.

116. CT, p. 229.

117. Unidentified. See Namkhai Norbu and Adriano Clemente, *The Supreme Source* (Ithaca, NY: Snow Lion Publications, 1999), appendix iv, p. 254.

> with himself abiding as the principal in the center, {88}
> along with the four teachers that are none other than himself,
> teaching the retinue of the individual families
> through intrinsic blessing,
> without explaining dharmas of speech.[118]

And the *Secret Array of Vidyā Tantra* states:

> The time when the saṃbhogakāya explains through its own essence
> is when the luminous supreme kaya appears.

The nirmāṇakāya's explanation through grammar and composition: Teacher Vajrasattva arrived through apparitional birth in the center of many stalks of lotus flowers in the place [called] Grove Mixed with Pure Mind. His peaceful mind faced the vajradhātu maṇḍala. Vajrasattva [of the vajradhātu maṇḍala] introduced him to the meaning according to the basis; Ratnasambhava introduced him to the sign according to the meaning; Amitābha introduced him to the example according to the symbol; and Amoghasiddhi explained the meaning grammatically according to the words.

From the age of eight until he was sixteen, Teacher Vajrasattva turned the inner wheel of pristine consciousness on the axle of wisdom; that is, he freed himself with the individually discerning pristine consciousness of impartial wisdom, {89} abiding without moving away from the dharmatā of the transcendent state.

From the age of sixteen until he was twenty-five, Teacher Vajrasattva turned the outer wheel of pristine consciousness on the axle of wisdom and engaged in benefiting others by emanating the six self-originated munis from his mind. With respect to the uncommon retinue, Garab Dorjé emanated from his brow and was appointed to be the *vidyādhara* of the buddhas. Guhyapati emanated from his nose and was assigned to be the suppliant. Mañjuśrī and Avalokiteśvara emanated from his two ears to explain the secret Dharma. Since the wheel of the Dharma

118. CT, p. 22.

of definitive meaning was turned through ascertaining the symbols and language in the three different divine places,[119] Teacher Vajrasattva freed others with his compassion. Then, having decided to pass into nirvāṇa, he bestowed all the texts of the aural lineage and the intimate instructions to the Mahācārya Garab Dorjé, advising, "Promulgate this in the future." After Garab Dorjé received the three last testaments,[120] {90} his misery was dispelled. The *Compendium of Tilakas Tantra* states:

> When I took apparitional birth from
> a great, blazing udumvara flower,
> the four rivers of empowerment
> in the maṇḍala of my mind were complete.
> Consequently, I obtained power over the pristine
> consciousness of realization
> and explained the definitive meaning in symbols and words
> three times.[121]

And the *Secret Array of Vidyā Tantra* states:

> When the nirmāṇakāya eloquently explained sentences,
> they were granted to compatible sentient beings.

1.2 The Symbolic Lineage of the Vidyādharas

The explanation of the way Mahācārya Garab Dorjé took birth in Jambudvīpa, was emanated by Śrī Vajrasattva, and appointed the *vidyādhara* of the buddhas to tame human beings: In Oḍḍiyāna, on the western side of India, there lived Bhikṣuṇī Sudharma, the daughter of

119. In the *Mirror of Key Points of the Profound Meaning*, p. 182, among the three places of the devas, the first place is the location of the teacher Child Inconceivable Sublime Appearances. The second place is the peak of the Blazing Volcano Charnel Ground, with the teacher Grimacing Youth. The third place is Gṛdhrakūṭa, with the teacher Buddha Kāśyapa the Elder. These three teachers are connected with the *Three Last Testaments of the Buddhas*.

120. *Three Last Testaments of the Buddhas*, NTY, vol. 3, pp. 295–304.

121. CT, pp. 229–30.

a prince named Uparāja and a princess named Illuminated Clearly (*gsal ba'i ldan ma*). Bhikṣuṇī Sudharma dwelled in concentration on Dhanakośa Island in the west. She dreamed that a white crystal man placed a crystal vase on her head, {91} conferring an empowerment. Nine months and ten days later, Sudharma gave birth from her right side to a child endowed with all the major and minor marks, and she was alarmed. "Who can this fatherless boy be other than a worldly ghost? Is he a worldly māra, or Brahmā, and so on? Who in the three realms will want him? Who has ever seen such an example? Alas, I have pure vows and wish to conquer existence. I shall be blamed for sexual misconduct, a grave offense." She concealed the infant in a pile of ashes. The earth shook, a great shower of flowers fell, and devas uttered the following benediction from the sky:

> I go for refuge to
> the Protector, Teacher, and Bhagavān,
> the naturally illuminated protector of the world.
> May we now strive for the vajra of space.

The ḍākinīs amassed a cloudbank of offerings, and the devas, nāgas, *yakṣas*, and so on, rained down sandalwood, saffron, and so on. {92} From all directions the worldly guardians beat on dharma drums, sounded conches, planted victory banners, raised pennants, and so on. The *ṛṣi* kings amassed immeasurable clouds of medicine. Having seen all this, Sudharma understood her child to be an emanation and requested his forbearance. She revived the child by washing him with a white silk and a finger bowl of scented water and milk. Then, like a lotus on the great ocean, he grew larger and taller than others.

For his name, the ḍākinīs called him Ashen Zombie (*ro lang thal mdog*). After he reached seven years of age, his knowledge arose naturally without training in many dharmas. He debated and conversed with the five hundred paṇḍitas of Oḍḍiyāna, but not one could answer his questions and not one could object to his replies. Thus, the paṇḍitas called him Mahācārya Prajñabhava. He is named Garab Dorjé because he pleased the king, and all the people of the country called him Happy Zombie (*ro langs bde ba*). These four names arise from the merit of the aspirations of the bodies of the four birthplaces,[122] where in past lives he was part of the inner retinue of the Teacher. {93}

After that, he remained in the samādhi of the transcendent state until he was thirty-two years of age on a mountain in the north called Brilliant Sun. After this, he left for the peak of Malaya, where he set in writing the precious *piṭaka*s of the teachings of the buddhas of the past and, in particular, he entrusted the 6,400,000 ślokas of the Great Perfection that were present in his mind to the ḍākinīs residing in the Source of the Ḍākinīs Cave. After this, the mahācārya dwelled in the Śitavana charnel ground.

At that time, in a city called Two Levels (*rim pa gnyis pa*) lived Mahācārya Mañjuśrīmitra, an expert in the five sciences, who was the child of a brahmin, Excellent Teacher, and his wife, Beautiful Clear Appearance. While residing and practicing in the Secret[123] Valley Charnel Ground, *Mañjuśrītīkṣṇa (*'jam dpal rnon po*) arrived in the sky and made a prediction, "Oh son of a good family, if you want the definitive meaning, go to the Śitavana charnel ground." {94} As soon as Mañjuśrīmitra heard this, he departed and met Garab Dorjé in person, prostrated to him, and requested to be accepted as his disciple. After his request was granted and Mañjuśrīmitra was taught the whole Dharma completely, Guru Garab Dorjé passed away at the head of the Dantik river without leaving any remains. Subsequently, Ācārya Mañjuśrīmitra sealed the whole of the textual lineage (*dpe brgyud*) under a rock marked with a crossed vajra to the northeast of Vajrāsana and then took residence in the Sosadvipa charnel ground.

At that time, in a city in China called Shokyam (*sho 'khyams*) lived Ācārya Śrī Siṃha, who was the son of a householder, Virtuous Mind, and his wife, Illuminated Mind. He was endowed with the qualities of a trained scholar. In the empty sky in the direction of the Golden Isle (*gser ling*), Avalokiteśvara arrived and gave Śrī Siṃha a prediction, "Oh fortunate son, if you want the definitive meaning, go to the Sosadvipa charnel ground in India!"

122. Apparitional birth, warmth and moisture birth, egg birth, and womb birth.

123. GC reads *bzang* rather than *gsang*.

Hearing this, Śrī Siṃha accomplished swift feet. On arriving he met Ācārya Mañjuśrīmitra, prostrated before him, circumambulated, and requested to be accepted as a disciple. {95} Ācārya Mañjuśrīmitra gave Śrī Siṃha the whole Dharma, along with the prediction for the text lineage, and departed without remains on top of the stūpa in that charnel ground. After this, Mahācārya Śrī Siṃha recovered the texts from the northeast of Vajrāsana, left for the Bodhi Tree in China, and concealed the text lineage.[124] He resided while in samādhi in the Granting Coolness (*bsil sbyin*) charnel ground.[125]

At that time in western India, in Elephant Ridge (*glang po sgang*), lived Mahācārya Vyemalamudra, the son of Princess Dharmabodhi, the daughter of King Dharmā Aśa.[126] At five years of age, his knowledge was self-born in all five sciences. {97} He and Ācārya Jñānasūtra went on a vacation to Naḍavanam (*'dam bu'i tshal*) to the west of Vajrāsana. In the sky above, Vajrasattva gave them a prediction, "Oh fortunate ones, if you want the definitive meaning of the result in a single lifetime, depart to the Bodhi Tree [in China]." Ācārya Vyemalamudra left and met Śrī Siṃha, who bestowed the aural lineages. Ācārya Vyemalamudra returned to India and resided in samādhi in the great charnel ground called Illumination (*snang byed*). Later, he was invited by King Indrabodhi and appointed to be one of the royal chaplains.

This concludes the symbolic lineage of *vidyādhara*s.

124. This is likely a reference to the Bodhi Tree at Guangxiao Temple, planted ca. 250 CE. This temple has several pagodas; one pagoda has over nine hundred niches.

125. GC gives *bsil byed bya ba*.

126. The following appears as an annotation in the underlying text: "Here, some claim that it was because Vyemalamudra was fatherless that his mother hid him in a sandpit. But as he did not die and his eyes were wide open, he was called *Bye ma la mu tra* (Mudrā in the Sand). Others claim that he was given this name because he knew how to debate the finest points of the Dharma. Those who make these assertions are just babbling and contradict the correct explanation found in the *Turquoise Writing*. Therefore, according to the prediction in the *Great Array of Ati* of 'the supreme scholar named "mudrin,"' *vyema* is translated as 'very great' (*rgya che*), and *mudrā* is translated as 'gesture' (*phyag rgya*), rendering *Vyemalamudra*. His ordination name is Vimalamitra, or Friend of the Immaculate (*dri med gshes gnyen*)."

1.3 The Aural Lineage of Esteemed Persons

At that time, Trisong Detsen (*khri strong lde'u btsan*), the king of Tibet, had built Glorious Samyé at Red Cliffs. Innumerable translators and paṇḍitas were involved in translations, yet he was dissatisfied. He thought, "I must bring a Dharma of buddhahood in one lifetime, in a single body, which surpasses cause and result, one more profound than these dharmas." The king's minister of Dharma, Nyang Tingzin Zangpo (*nyang ting 'dzin bzang po*), said, "Oh lord, King Indrabodhi has five hundred paṇḍita royal chaplains. {97} Among them, the one who is [both] a scholar and a siddha should be invited."

The trio of translators, Kawa Paltsek (*ka ba pal brtsegs*), Cokro Lui Gyaltsen (*cog ro klu'i rgyal mtshan*), and Ma Rinchen Chog (*rma rin chen mchog*), were sent to invite Vimalamitra with gold powder and many gold ingots as gifts. The translators offered gifts to King Indrabodhi. In return for the gifts, they asked for a favor, "Among your paṇḍitas, there is one who is a scholar and has attained siddhi. Please let him travel to Tibet." When the king summoned the assembly, [the three translators,] looking down the upper row of two hundred and fifty and up the lower row of two hundred and fifty, knew that Vimalamitra had been summoned.

Vimalamitra gathered his collection of Dharma into one *kāpāla*,[127] which was four finger-lengths long, and carrying this, he departed. On arriving in Tibet, he was greeted with great fanfare. He translated and taught the outer and inner dharmas. In particular, he taught three of the Tilaka cycles to the king and his sons, as well as to Nyang. Having satisfied them, Vimalamitra departed for the Five-Peaked Mountain in China.

Next, Nyang Tingzin Zangpo {98} left for the White Cliffs of Zho (*gzho'i brag dkar*) in Üru. After Dorjé Legpa caused a hailstorm in Kham, he was taxed five hundred bushels of wheat by Nyang, who used the proceeds to construct the temple of Hayagriva in Zhva. He divided the Tilaka cycle into the textual lineage and the aural lineage, concealing

127. A human cranium carried by tantric practitioners.

the textual lineage as a treasure. To prevent the decline of this aural lineage, he saw Bé Lödro Wangchuk (*sbas blo gros dbang phyug*) of Phanyul as a fortunate one. When Nyang bestowed the teaching, Bé Lödro Wangchuk was forbidden to promulgate it beyond a single lineage holder, saying, "You may entrust this to a single suitable recipient," and applied the command seal. Bé Lödro Wangchuk saw that Drom Rinchen Bar was a suitable recipient for instruction and bestowed the aural lineage with the command seal. Dromtön Rinchen Bar saw that Dangma Lhungi Gyaltsen was the owner of this teaching and bestowed it upon him. After the protector Vajrasādhu gave Dangma a prediction, the latter retrieved the treasure texts. After keeping them secret for twelve years, Dangma went in search of a recipient for the teachings.

Che Thubpé Wangpo (*lce thub pa'i dbang po*) and Khyungmo Za Legma (*khyung mo bza' legs ma*)[128] of Nyangro[129] gave birth to the faithful Chetsun Sengé Wangchuk, who left in search of the Dharma. {99} Dangma and Chetsun encountered each other in an uninhabited valley among steep mountains in Tsang. Dangma saw that Chetsun was the destined one and bestowed upon him the different classes of the aural lineage.[130]

Chetsun saw that Zhongpa Repa (*shong pa ras pa*) was a destined one and taught him. Zhongpa Repa saw that Zabtön Chöbar was a fortunate one and taught him. Zabtön Chöbar recognized that Dampa Gyertön was the owner of the instructions and taught him. Dampa Gyertön taught Kyemé Jokyab. Kyemé Jokyab taught Gyertön Jo Mé. This teaching was heard by Nyentön Sherab Tsemo from the two previous teachers: the close lineage was given to Nyentön by Gyertön Jo Mé and the long lineage was given to him individually by both Kyemé Jokyab and Gyertön Jo Mé. Nyentön went to Ü and upon meeting Rinpoché Yönten Gangpa saw that he was a destined one and bestowed all

128. Khyung is an important Tibetan clan. *Khyung mo bza'* means "Lady of the Khyung clan."

129. *Nyang ro*. In GC, this is spelled *Myang ro*. Myang is the area of Tsang province where the Lce clan homesteaded during the pre-Buddhist period. See Smith, *Self-Arisen Vidyā Tantra*, p. 28n13.

130. This refers to the written and unwritten aural lineages.

the instructions. Nyentön released the command seal, saying, "When I left Yar, I left behind my texts, however, since you understand all my instructions, you should go benefit migrating beings," and entrusted him with the lineage. Rinpoché Yönten Gangpa became renowned for holding buddhahood in his hand. Rinpoché then recognized Lama Namkha Dorjé as a destined one {100} and gave him the complete teaching. The sublime guru, Kumarāja, petitioned Lama Namkha Dorjé, who bestowed the introductions and the supporting texts in their entirety. Lama Namkha Dorjé said to his younger brother, "This teaching of the aural lineage must be entrusted to Kumarāja," and so it was given to him in its entirety.

These are the alternate lineages: Rinpoché Yönten Gangpa taught it to Lama Tsezhing (*bla ma rtse zhing*). Lama Rinpoché (Kumarāja) requested the latter for the teaching. Yönten Gangpa taught Tönpa Rinchen Sengé (*ston pa rin chen seng ge*). Tönpa Rinchen Sengé taught the fortunate Chökyi Sherab (*chos kyi shes rab*). Chökyi Sherab taught Lama Kumarāja. Further, in the Sun Valley Encampment Nyangtö in Tsang, the sublime lama requested the lineage stemming from the great mahāsiddha, Löppon Yeshé Gon (*slob dpon ye shes mgon*). Having experienced many hardships, the river of instruction was again complete.

The great *vidyādhara* [Kumarāja] entrusted this to me, saying, "You must benefit sentient beings," adding to a great sense of joy. This concludes the lineage of esteemed persons.

As such, from the original protector up to the yogi himself, since there is no breach of samaya, no deception in the instruction, {101} no deviation or mistake in the practice, no interruption in benefiting others, no interruption in the measure of liberation, and no interruption in the line of blessing, this lineage is superior to others.

2. *How the Instruction Is Bestowed*

There are three topics in the intimate instruction of the key points of how the instruction is bestowed: The characteristics of the ācārya who bestows the instruction are that, outwardly, their mind has been freed by hearing and reflection; inwardly, their qualities have been perfected by practice; and secretly, their conduct benefits others through unification. The characteristics of the disciple who receives the instruction are that, outwardly, the instruction of the tantras, *āgamas*, and *upadeśas* are not to be explained to the unsuitable; inwardly, the instructions of the introductions of the aural lineage are not to be set down in writing; and secretly, the intimate instructions of the mind lineage are not to be explained to the talkative.

3. The Introduction for Realization and Liberation

There are five topics in the instructions concerning the introduction for realization and liberation: (1) confirming the basis, path, and result; (2) binding the key points with the six lamps; (3) summarizing the essentials as pristine consciousness; {102} (4) planting the nail with the five inscriptions; and (5) setting the command seal through high value.

3.1 Confirming the Basis, Path, and Result

There are three topics: (1) the basis as one's own nature, (2) explaining the path as the explicit instruction (*dmar khrid*), and (3) explaining the result as the mode of liberation.

3.1.1 The Basis

There are three topics: (1) the original generic basis, (2) the basis of the liberation of Samantabhadra, (3) and the basis of the delusion of ignorant sentient beings.

3.1.1.1 The Original Generic Basis

Prior to realization arising as buddhas and nonrealization arising as sentient beings, the field—empty dharmadhātu—opened up, resembling the depths of pure sky; limpid and still, resembling the depths of the ocean; and clear and open, resembling the surface of a mirror. The core in the dimension of dharmatā, the vidyā that appropriates the basis[131] exists as essence, nature, and compassion. That does not impede saṃsāra. The space of [vidyā] arising as saṃsāra is uninterrupted, resembling camphor. That does not impede nirvāṇa. The space of [vidyā] arising as nirvāṇa is uninterrupted, resembling camphor.[132] Though its essence is not delineated in any way, it arises in many ways due to conditions. There are no flaws in the basis. {103} As a mere basis of arising, since it produces whatever is desired, the basis abides as the source of everything, resembling a wish-fulfilling gem. The *Universal Tilaka* states:

> Prior to producing and arising,
> Changeless Light, the original protector,
> is present as the great source of everything,
> like the sky, the ocean, a jewel, and camphor.[133]

And:

> Prior to producing and arising,
> when realization did not produce buddhas
> and nonrealization did not produce sentient beings,
> prior to the existence of either,
> Changeless Light, the original protector,
> attained buddhahood that was naturally perfected by nature.
> [Changeless Light] isn't annihilated, his body is luminosity,
> and he isn't permanent, because his body has no substance,
> abiding in the manner of a rainbow in space,
> present as the source of everything,

131. "Vidyā that appropriates the basis," also termed "unripened vidyā," refers to vidyā that has appropriated a body of the six realms. It is defined in the *Lamp that Summarizes Vidyā*, pp. 225–26, as that which "generates all consciousness when abiding in the body and abides as mere clarity." "Mere clarity" refers to the "light" that exists in various amounts in the bodies of all sentient beings of six realms.

132. The comparison made here is that one thing can be harmful in one context and beneficial in another. Just as camphor is said to be harmful for cold diseases and beneficial for hot diseases, the non-recognition of the basis results in saṃsāra, while the recognition of the basis results in nirvāṇa.

133. Unattested.

the basis of entities,
free from falling into limitations,
abiding as effortlessly inseparable.[134]

Further, since the essence of this self-originated pristine consciousness of vidyā has always been naturally perfected, it is like a jewel. Though it is delineated as neither saṃsāra nor nirvāṇa, through the condition of realization and nonrealization, it does not obstruct the space of arising as saṃsāra or nirvāṇa. Like camphor, {104} it is neither beneficial nor harmful; through the condition of hot and cold illnesses camphor arises unobstructedly as either beneficial or harmful. While vidyā itself is not established as anything—however it may seem through conditions when it is made the basis of arising—ultimately, it does not change into good or bad and is called "the reality of the basis."

3.1.1.2 The Basis of the Liberation of Samantabhadra

The basis of the liberation of Samantabhadra {105} is that he attained buddhahood by recognizing himself directly through the basis itself. There are three self-originated dharmas for Śrī Samantabhadra: (1) His buddhahood arises within the state of the intimate instruction that does not arise from scripture. He knew this without a guru teaching a scripture. (2) The buddhahood that did not arise from mind was the buddhahood he knew by himself. He himself knew the basis in absence of a body, voice, and mind. (3) Since the result that did not arise from a cause was established in himself, he attained buddhahood. He knew the basis himself without the basis being a condition for the three kāyas. Further, since those three pristine consciousnesses abiding in the basis are the power of the wisdom of his own knowledge, the result was born as the three kāyas in him.

There are three bases of liberation in the liberation of Samantabhadra: {104} The basis of liberation of the field is self-recognition through self-appearance. The basis of liberation of the body is the self-

134. Unattested.

recognition of self-appearance as the rūpakāya. After the pristine consciousness of omniscience arose as the basis of liberation of the mind, it self-liberated. The *Universal Tilaka* states:

> Since the self-originated maṇḍala self-appeared
> simultaneously with self-recognition,
> the connate pristine consciousness arose.
> Since I am the immaculate dharmakāya,
> the pristine consciousness of omniscience arose.
> The dharmakāya recognized its self-arising cognizance.[135]

Further, since that *svabhāvakāya*, naturally perfected buddhahood by nature, knew and realized itself without stirring from its own state (*rang mal*), the dharmakāya buddha, Samantabhadra, attained awakening in the original basis.[136]

3.1.1.3 *The Basis of the Delusion of Ignorant Sentient Beings*

The basis of delusion of ignorant sentient beings is that they are deluded through not recognizing the appearance of the basis. Further, the basis of delusion of objects is becoming deluded by not recognizing luminosity is present as their own appearance. The basis of delusion of karma is becoming deluded from not recognizing the rūpakāya of the five lights of the basis as their own bodies. The basis of delusion of the mind is not recognizing the vidyā of the basis. The *Universal Tilaka* states: {106}

> Why is dharmatā valid as the basis of delusion of the field?
> It is insentient and appears[137] inert.

135. Unattested.

136. This passage can best be understood in reference to a very important controversy raised by Haribhadra in his *Abhisamayālaṃkārāloka*; see Gareth Sparham, *Abhisamayālaṃkāra with Vṛtti and Ālokā*, vol. 4, pp. 247–65. Should the dharmakāya be understood to be the same as the *svabhāvakāya* or are these two kāyas distinct? In Haribhadra's presentation, the *svabhāvakāya* is understood to be ultimate truth, while the three kāyas—dharmakāya, saṃbhogakāya, and nirmāṇakāya—are understood to be the correct relative truth.

137. Following UT, reading *snang* for *gnas*.

Why is vidyā valid as the basis of delusion of the mind?
It belongs to the same genre as mere cognizance.
The five lights are acceptable as the basis of delusion of a body
because those belong to the same genre of color and shape . . .[138]
Primordial stirring is deluded as mind.
The creator is "I" and "mine."
There is delusion when the apprehended object and apprehending subject arise.
Time is understood as two kinds.
The result is the gradual formation of existence,
the universe and inhabitants from the Ābhāsvara devas on down.[139]

From the first period of the basis, the middle period of the appearance of the basis arose. Because its own state was not recognized, the [final] period of deluded appearance is perpetuated. From among the formation of the universe and inhabitants of the three realms and the six classes of beings as explained in this tantra, the formation stage of the container universe is as follows:

At that time, through the conceptuality of the apprehended object and apprehending subject,
the five lights of the nature lacked the power to be clear.
Because of traces in the five reflections,[140]
like the formation of ice on a lake or skin on curd,
the details of the four continents and Sumeru appear.
From the contents is born the cosmic egg,
grass, trees, forests, medicinal herbs, and flowers,
and there is birth from moisture and warmth.

138. UT, p. 325.

139. The remainder of this passage is unattested.

140. Following UT, p. 329, reading *gzugs brnyan* for *gzugs sogs*.

As such, the period when the container universe
is differentiated is the middle period.[141] {107}

This tantra continues with the inhabitants:

Similar to the wind moving through empty sky,
the mind (*yid*) is a great wind that goes everywhere.
The cosmic egg is seen with the union of the eye;
it is known to be beautiful by union with the mind;
a passionate mind arises through the union of the gaze;
vidyā and mind abide together,
ripening individually as male and female sentient beings.
This is egg birth among the four kinds of birth . . .
After that, birth from a womb was produced,
and thus, the Sahaloka was gradually formed.
Afflictions coarsened and the result was bad.
Finally, in the end, there were hells.[142]

3.1.2 Explaining the Path as the Explicit Instruction

There are three topics in explaining the path as the explicit instruction: (1) the formation of the body of traces, (2) the way mind and pristine consciousness abide, and (3) the way the instruction is illustrated with introductions.

3.1.2.1 The Formation of the Body of Traces

The *Universal Tilaka* states:

First, the formation of the body begins with the eyes.
Subsequently, the whole body is generated.
Two nāḍīs arise from the eyes,

141. UT, p. 153.

142. UT, pp. 154–55. Here Longchenpa paraphrases and abbreviates this passage, but in the *Mirror of the Profound Meaning*, p. 245, he provides the passage in its complete form.

> becoming a cluster of nāḍīs.
> After that, the whole body is generated.[143]
> The branches of the nāḍīs arise.
> At that time the functional organs form individually,
> the inner viscera, the heart, lungs, and so on, {108}
> which is the way the composite body forms.

In the formation (*chags*), development (*bskyed*), and perpetuation (*gnas*) of the body, first, four things merge: the white and red bindus of the father and mother, and the vāyu and mind of the gandharva who is nearby. During the first week, two eyes form in the center of the triangular cluster of nāḍīs in the center of the oval *arbuda*, which is one-third the size of a mustard seed. During the second week, the pure part of blood forms in the eastern nāḍī, inside the oblong *kalala*, which is one-hundredth the size of a horse hair. During the third week, the pure part of flesh forms in the southern nāḍī inside the lumpy *peśī*. During the fourth week, the pure part of heat forms in the western nāḍī inside the round *ghana*. During the fifth week, the three nāḍīs and the four cakras form inside the hardened *khara*. During the sixth week, the Viṣṇu tadpole forms, which is the size of the width of the mother's four fingers held together (*chag*). During the seventh week, the buds of the limbs form in the tortoise phase, which is the size of the mother's fist and extended thumb. During the eighth week, the sense organs and all the limbs form in the Viṣṇu tortoise, which is the size of the length between the mother's outstretched thumb and her pinky.

The development of the body is the developmental maturation of form through the pure essence of the food the mother has eaten, because the vāyu has entered the central channel [of the fetus], completing the development of the body in nine months and ten days. The *Universal Tilaka* states:

> The way nutriment generates the body[144]

143. This line is a deliberate repetition.

144. UT reads */lus stobs gso byed bcud kyi chags lugs/*.

is through the connection of both mother and child at the
navel.
Development begins from the navel,
developing strength and brilliance.[145]

Then, following birth, the existence of the body is governed by the increase, duration, and decline of the trio of nāḍīs, vāyus, and bindus. The nāḍīs are the support of the body, which in turn supports the bindus and the vāyus. Among the nāḍīs are three principal nāḍīs, four cakras, and ten million minor nāḍīs. The *Universal Tilaka* states:

Though the four nāḍī cakras of the nāḍī knots[146] of the body
have many connections like a network of wheels,
the three nāḍīs of pristine consciousness that generate the
three kāyas
are supreme, very straight in the manner of pillars.

Concerning the nāḍī petals, there are sixty-four in the navel, eight in the heart center, sixteen in the throat, and thirty-two petals in the crown. Innumerable minor nāḍīs branch off from those.

Concerning the vāyu, there are both major and minor movements in the nāḍīs. {110} There are five vāyus that perform functions: The lifting vāyu exists in the four limbs and generates the strength of flesh and bone. The vāyu that generates luster and brilliance exists in the brow and generates the strength of blood and lymph. The fire-accompanying vāyu exists in the stomach and digests food. The vāyu that separates the pure and the impure exists both above and below, spreading the pure part of the food throughout the body and eliminating the waste products. The vāyu of the compassionless eon exists in the heart inseparably with vidyā and performs the function of liberating saṃsāra into dharmatā.

Bodhicitta moves inside the nāḍīs: The ultimate bindu moves inside the *lalanā*, the relative bindu moves inside the *rasanā*, and the natural

145. UT, p. 443.

146. Following SDP, p. 384, reading *lus kyi rgya mdud* for *lus kyi rgyab mdun*.

bindu moves inside the central nāḍī. For women, it is the opposite.[147] The white bindu generates the brain and marrow, which in turn generates the bone, adipose tissue, tendons, and ligaments. The red bindu generates muscle, which in turn generates lymph, which in turn generates the skin, which in turn generates the hair and pores. The key point of those is that when the pure part increases, the body is attractive, and there is no white hair or wrinkles, which occur when the pure part decreases.

3.1.2.2 The Way Mind and Pristine Consciousness Abide

Though the way the mind and pristine consciousness {111} abide is not differentiated in other dharmas, the special instructions in this Dharma differentiate the respective locations, paths, doorways, and results of both mind and pristine consciousness.

3.1.2.2.1 The Location of Pristine Consciousness

Pristine consciousness is located on the three rims in the maṇḍala of the precious heart center as the peaceful deities, and its radiance is located in the brain as the wrathful deities. *Chanting the Names of Mañjuśrī* states:

> A glorious knot of blazing light.[148]

And the *Universal Tilaka* states:

> In the celestial mansion of the precious heart center,
> the kāya is tiny, the size of a sesame seed,
> abiding as complete, within a sphere of five lights.[149]

And:

147. For women, the right and left nāḍīs are reversed.

148. CNMa, 6a.

149. Unattested.

In the mansion of the eight-faceted gem,
the kāyas and pristine consciousness are like a lamp,
naturally perfected, not abiding elsewhere.[150]

Those [kāyas and pristine consciousnesses] exist in the center of the intrinsic radiance of the five pristine consciousnesses of vidyā, like the simile of a peacock egg. The empty essence is similar to the round and transparent shape of the egg. The clear nature swirls as the five lights, similar to the rippled albumen inside the egg. Cognizant compassion is like the consciousness of the chick inside the egg. The *Blazing Body of the Charnel Ground Tantra* states:

Essence, nature, and compassion
resemble the example of a peafowl egg.{112}
The form of the shape is the dharmakāya;
the rippled albumen[151] is the five lights,
showing the example of the saṃbhogakāya;
and when the pea chick hatches,
the example of the nirmāṇakāya is shown.[152]

The path of pristine consciousness is the nāḍī that runs from the heart center up to the eyes, which is like a white silk thread, devoid of blood and lymph. The *Universal Tilaka* states:

Connecting the precious [heart center] to the ocean,
the smooth, white, hollow, empty nāḍī
is not filled with bindu or blood.
It is explained to be the path of pristine consciousness,
in which great pristine consciousness always moves.[153]

150. Unattested.

151. Here Longchenpa reads *chu ris* for CGT *chos nyid.*

152. CGT, p. 833.

153. UT, pp. 445–46.

The doorway of pristine consciousness: all the universe and inhabitants manifest as the light of one's own radiance through the lamp of the watery far-reaching lasso.

The result of pristine consciousness is the three kāyas that are complete, naturally perfected in oneself.

The location of mind is the nāḍī of the lungs. This nāḍī, which is the size of a stalk of wheat, connects the lungs to the heart, where the vāyu comes into contact with the radiance of pristine consciousness. The doorway of the mind is the individual nāḍī petals from the lungs that give rise to the consciousness of the five sense gates. The doorways are the mouth and nostrils and the pure essence of the sense organs that support the appearance of the objects of desire of the five sense gates. The function of the mind is accumulating karma and traces from the apprehended object and the apprehending subject. The result of the mind is establishing saṃsāra. Since the essence of the mind is the radiance of pristine consciousness coming into contact with the vāyu, concepts engage objects. The radiance of pristine consciousness, like a sighted paraplegic, is mounted on the movement of vāyu, like an ambulatory blind horse, from which the consciousness of the objects of the outer and inner group of six arises in the form of mental factors (*sems byung*). Since the mental factors are the intrinsic radiance of vidyā, those are flickering (*mi bkra dgu bkra*), and since those are stirred by vāyu, those are incessant (*mi 'gyu dgu 'gyu*). The *Universal Tilaka* states:

> Mind and pristine consciousness
> are neither the same nor different.
> They are phenomena that are difficult to differentiate.
> The mind is the potential of pristine consciousness.
> The basis of the mind is pristine consciousness.
> Therefore, since mind and pristine consciousness
> are both the same and different,
> there is so-called "liberation" and "nonliberation."[154]

And the *Blazing Body of the Charnel Ground Tantra* states:

154. UT, p. 445.

> The essence of the mind is pristine consciousness,
> which arises as the potential of subject and object.
> Since [pristine consciousness] uses the breath as the mount, it meets conditions[155]
> that increase dualistic concepts.
> The place is the abode of the windy house.
> The path is the throat through which [the breath] moves.
> The door arises as the five[156] doors of desire.
> The fault[157] is the arising of diverse concepts.[158]
> The function is grasping subject and object as "mine." {114}

Garab Dorjé's *Golden Rosary* states:

> The connection of the gem to the lamp is the size of a silk thread and white.
> The connection of the gem to the airy one is the size of a stalk of wheat and red.
> The connection of the airy one connected to the doorway [the throat] is the size of a section of bamboo.

Thus, the radiance of the naturally perfected nature, pristine consciousness, arises from the two nāḍīs that are connected from the heart to the eyes. The intrinsic radiance of compassion in the two nāḍīs, which are connected from the heart to the lungs, arises as the mind, because it comes into contact with the vāyu.

3.1.2.3 The Way the Instruction Is Illustrated with Introduction

There are three topics in the way the instruction is illustrated with introductions: (1) the diagram section arranged on the ground, (2) the

155. These three lines and the final line are not attested in CGT.

156. Reading *lnga* for CGT *gsum*.

157. Reading CGT *rkyon* for *rkyen*.

158. CGT, p. 829.

symbol section shown in space, and (3) the meaning section that abides in oneself.

3.1.2.3.1 *The Diagram Section*

Outline the center and the sides. There are three circles: The center circle is arranged with five lights, and the middle is blue. The inner circle is red with twelve lotus petals—the eastern petal is white, the southern petal is yellow, the western petal is red, the northern petal is green, and the intermediate petals are blue. The outer rim is beautified with sixteen petals. Thus, the arrangement of the twenty-eight segments are the purities of the deities of the perfect basis.

3.1.2.3.2 *The Symbol Section Arranged in Space*

The symbol cycle arranged in space is "Further, show the symbols to the eyes {115} and pour the voice into the ears." The *Abbreviated Tantra*[159] states:

> *Vidyādhara* retinue,
> show the symbols of the corresponding direction
> to those I have accepted as followers
> and confirm the definitive meaning with the voice.[160]

The disciple is placed on a suitable cushion to the left of the guru. Pick up the crystal and recite this:

> Śrī Vajrasattva said, "Do not ask me. Instead, ask the Vajrasattva Mirror."

The *Uprooting Saṃsāra Tantra* states:

159. Unidentified.

160. *Sdud pa'i rgyud*, unidentified.

> If one does not know the kāya that transcends phenomena, look[161] at one's cognizance! If one does not know the example illustrating that, look at the Vajrasattva Mirror! If one does not know the sign of that[162] abiding within oneself, look at the lamp of bodhicitta.[163]

The *Moistened Ground* states:

> In the heart of limitless light arises a precious stūpa with five tiers. On each tier are the complete five families with retinues. The great body relic inseparable from the Buddha settles, and that actually settles in the left hand. After that becomes a mirror of pristine consciousness, {116} looking, realization, and liberation arise simultaneously, becoming the mirror of the knowable."[164]

Next, with their eyes, the disciple raises the diagram section into the space of the crystal. Having shown this vividly as a direct perception of the sense organ, [the guru says:]

> Oh fortunate one, the essence of the self-originated pristine consciousness of vidyā in the center of your heart is empty, its nature is clear, and it manifests as the intrinsic radiance of the kāyas and pristine consciousnesses, which is nondual with compassion. Since one looks at the symbol of the three kāyas abiding as the great natural perfection, the three-rimmed maṇḍala of the perfect basis, and since this is understood with recognition and knowing, doubts are eliminated. The *Universal Tilaka* states:

161. Both BGB and Tsham read *dris shig* in this and the following line.

162. Both BGB and Tsham read *sangs rgyas kyi sku*, "kāya of the Buddha."

163. *Uprooting Saṃsāra Tantra*, BGB, pp. 15–16; Tsham, p. 71. This tantra is found in the mahāyoga section of Tsham.

164. *Gzhi sbags*, unidentified.

> In the center of the maṇḍala of the self-originated three kāyas
> are two kāyas of limitless light,
> the Samantabhadra couple abiding as the dharmakāya.
> The inner rim is the kāya of the brilliant rainbow,
> abiding as the kāya of couples of the five families.
> The outer rim is the emanated retinue,
> abiding as the sixteen nirmāṇakāya bodhisattvas.[165]

[*Chanting the Names of Mañjuśrī* states:]

> Sixteen are twice halved.[166]
> The limbless[167] is beyond calculation.[168]

3.1.2.3.3 The Meaning Section

In the meaning section, there are three topics introducing what abides in oneself: (1) introducing the examples, (2) introducing the proofs, {117} and (3) introducing the meanings.

3.1.2.3.3.1 Introduction of the Examples

There are four in the examples: (1) the introduction of the crystal for the dharmakāya, (2) the introduction of the mask for the saṃbhogakāya, (3) the introduction of the house of light for the nirmāṇakāya, and (4) the

165. Unattested.

166. Garab Dorjé clarifies these two lines in *Illuminating the Meaning of the Mañjuśrīnāma-saṃgīti*, 59a, lines 4–7: "There are two meanings for 'Sixteen are twice halved.' Since each saṃbhogakāya is surrounded by two male and two female bodhisattvas, the clusters in the four directions are the retinue. Further, 'Sixteen' refers to the sixteen male and female bodhisattvas. The first 'halved' means they are divided into male and female. The second 'halved' means surrounding the saṃbhogakāya in groups of four."

167. Dharmakāya.

168. CNMa, 7b, line 5.

introduction of the heart of the sun for the inseparability of the three kāyas.[169]

3.1.2.3.3.1.1 *Introduction of the Crystal*

Place a Vajrasattva crystal on the left eye of a person of pure karma and say:

> Oh, all of you fortunate suitable recipients, this mind mirror is not the actual dharmakāya; however, understand that example as a simile. Just as there is no outside or inside in this exemplar, one must understand there is no outside or inside in the dharmakāya. Just as there is no front or back in this exemplar, one must understand there is no front or back in the dharmakāya. Just as this exemplar is pellucid, one must understand that the dharmakāya is pellucid. Just as the clarity of the five lights is without conditions because there is no inside [or outside] within this exemplar, the rūpakāya must be understood as the core of interiorized clarity, the pristine consciousness of natural perfection within the pellucid dharmakāya.[170] Just as the five lights are able to arise externally from the inside that is not an inside, one must understand that the two rūpakāyas are able to appear from the dharmakāya to those to be tamed.[171]

Thus, the pristine consciousness of one's vidyā is introduced as the dharmakāya. The *Last Testament* states: {118}

169. These four introductions are the subject matter of UT, chapter 86, pp. 448–51, and are paraphrased based on the chapter.

170. UT, p. 449, line 2: "Just as the five lights are clear without conditions when there is no inside or outside—the three kāyas abide as interiorized clarity in the state of pellucid dharmakāya—it must be understood that emptiness has a core of pristine consciousness."

171. This introduction is a paraphrase of the introduction found in UT, pp. 448–49.

When the simile of the crystal is demonstrated,
the sight of that is called "the meaning of suchness."[172]

3.1.2.3.3.1.2 Introduction of the Mask

To generate understanding of the way the self-appearing saṃbhogakāya youthful vase body arises, the guru dons bone ornaments and the disciples raise a mirror to their right eyes. Recite the introduction:

Oh, fortunate ones!
The kāya of pristine consciousness is self-originated.
Pellucid emptiness is the kāya of space,
the kāya without birth, death, or change.

The *Explanatory Tantra* states:

> When the mirror is shown to the mask, just as the mirror is pure and clear, dharmatā is pure and clear. Just as the reflection inside a mirror is apparent yet without inherent existence, the five kāyas in the dimension of empty dharmatā are apparent yet without inherent existence.[173]

And:

The kāya is tiny, the size of a sesame seed,
abiding as complete within a sphere of five lights.[174]

> As such, the radiance of the forty-two peaceful deities in the heart center abides within oneself. Though the kāyas of fifty-eight wrathful deities in the brain are not larger than a seed, their dimension in the bardo is equal with space, the size of Sumeru, {119} the size of a large house, or the size of

172. *Zhal chems*, unidentified.

173. UT, p. 449.

174. Unattested.

one's body, arising and filling space. At that time, one must recognize one's appearances as the rūpakāya.

After that, one must shut all windows. When the sun sets on the peak of Sumeru, introduce the transcendent state of the interiorized clarity of pristine consciousness. To engage in cultivating the sun, introduce the nāḍī path that connects the *śrīvatsa* (*dpal gyi be'u*) to the lamp.[175] Raise a mirror into a sun ray to introduce the time saṃsāra and nirvāṇa turn their back to each other. Roll the mirror to introduce the appearance of the basis. Press the nāḍī, play music, and roll the mirror to introduce sound, light, and rays. Further:

> From the self-appearance of the five lights within the bardo of dharmatā, like a mirage on the summer plain, the intrinsic sound of dharmatā is similar to the rumbling of one thousand peals of thunder, and the rays resemble a rain of weapons. Recognize the sound as one's own sound, the light as one's own light, and the rays as one's own rays!

Further, for those of limited faith in the present day, there is the introduction from the pristine consciousness that illuminates the interior and the nāḍī, the introduction to cause cognizance to become senseless through pressing, and the introduction to the appearance of appearances through sound, light, and rays.

3.1.2.3.3.1.3 The Introduction of the Union of the House of Light for the Nirmāṇakāya

The introduction of the union of the house of light for the nirmāṇakāya {120} illustrates the unceasing mode of arising of compassion. Focus the eyes on the conjunction of the light of a sun ray and the mirror and

175. The term *śrīvatsa*, often rendered as "eternal knot," symbolically refers to the location of vidyā in the heart center. In other contexts, it is one of the eighty minor marks of the Buddha, in this case, the one found on his chest.

introduce the union of the intrinsic radiance of the heart center arising in the far-reaching lasso. The *Universal Tilaka* states:

> Just as a mirror is pure and clear, the lamp of water is pure dharmatā. The five kāyas, which do not move their hands, appearing as light in the mirror, are the proof pristine consciousness just as it is, the nirmāṇakāya.[176]

3.1.2.3.3.1.4 The Introduction of the Disk of the Sun

The introduction of the disk of the sun for the inseparability of the three kāyas: Look at the disc of the sun through a veil of a dyed gauze sieve that is at the proper tension. When one sees multicolored rays emanate inside of a dimension of five lights and chains of bindus, this is illustrated with four unwritten symbols: The heart of the sun is the example of dharmakāya. The five lights are the example of the saṃbhogakāya. The light rays are the example of the nirmāṇakāya. Those three gathered into one are the example of the inseparability of the kāyas and pristine consciousnesses. The *Blazing Body of the Charnel Ground Tantra* states: {121}

> The simile is the heart of the sun.
> The heart of the sun is the example of the dharmakāya.
> The darkness of the six realms is removed
> by the various light rays that shine from the sun.
> The dharmakāya is nonconceptual and clear.
> The saṃbhogakāya experiences ceaseless wisdom.
> The compassion of the nirmāṇakāya releases affliction.
> Those three different[177] kāyas are a single state.[178]

The *Universal Tilaka* states:

176. This is a very rough paraphrase of UT, p. 449.

177. Reading CGT *mtha' dag* for *tha dad*.

178. CGT, p. 827.

> Just as light rays are not impeded in the heart of the sun, the dharmakāya arises adorned with the two kāyas. Just as the heart of the sun and its light rays are inseparable, since the three kāyas and pristine consciousness have never been separable, in reality I explain the inseparability of the dharmakāya.[179]

3.1.2.3.3.2 Introduction of the Proofs

The introduction of the proofs is the reasoning concerning pristine consciousness having always existed as naturally perfected luminosity in oneself. Since the lamp of bodhicitta is shown to exist in oneself, one has confidence. Moreover, the recognition of the pristine consciousness existing within oneself that arises in the bardo is illustrated with the introduction of the appearance of the basis. That also severs the thread that connects the body and mind, the inert and the sentient. The appearances of this life subside, and until the bardo of existence has arisen, there is the proof of the appearance of the trio of sound, light, and rays that arise in the bardo of dharmatā in three moments, six moments, and so on. {122} Since the sound of an elephant's trumpet is introduced to the ear, one has confidence that sound is an intrinsic sound. Since one presses the lamp of water with the hands, one sees the lamp of bodhicitta, and one has confidence that the light is intrinsic light.

The *Aural Lineage Commentary* states:

> The *śrīvatsa* and the lamp are connected by a nāḍī.
> The lamp is the door of self-arising dharmatā.
> The appearance manifests by covering the window.[180]

Since one directs the lamp of water [covered] by gauze at the sun, one easily sees the light rays of pristine consciousness arise. Since one is

179. This is an expanded paraphrase of the passage in UT, p. 304, on the introduction of the three kāyas as inseparable.

180. *Snyan brgyud ti ka*, unlocated.

confident that the rays are intrinsic rays, there are three proofs. Further, when the mother and child luminosity meet, all the light vibrates and throbs. The rays shine like sun rays of weapons. Within these rays, the intrinsic sound of dharmatā becomes like the rumble of one thousand thunders, which are understood to be a self-appearance.

3.1.2.3.3.3 Introduction of the Meaning

Next is the introduction. The three kāyas dwell inseparably inside the *śrīvatsa* in one's heart. The celestial mansion of pristine consciousness is recognized through the introduction with the example, one is confident about this introduction because of the introduction of the proof, and one ascertains that it exists within oneself through the introduction of the meaning. {123} Since this is confirmed with words, one should distinguish the trio of example, proof, and meaning existing presently in oneself and arising in the bardo later on. The *Universal Tilaka* states:

> The luminosity in the dimension of mind
> resembles a lamp in a vase.
> Unchanging pristine consciousness
> is the buddhahood[181] of the undeluded basis,
> the sublime meaning pristine consciousness.
> The mirror of great pristine consciousness
> is the unfabricated dharma,[182]
> the sublime example pristine consciousness.
> The thumb-sized maṇḍala of light
> is the unchanging view,[183]
> explained to be the proof pristine consciousness.[184]

Since a person who has obtained the introductions practices according to the explanation, there is no ground of deviation, and the self-

181. Following SLB, p. 366, reading *sangs rgyas* for *ye shes*.

182. Following SLB, p. 366, reading *chos nyid* for *chos yin*.

183. Omitted in SLB.

184. Unattested.

appearing maṇḍala arises. Since there is no ground for divergence, the mother and child dharmatā merge. Because that is the case, later, once the mother and child luminosity merge, if one does not have an experience resembling meeting with a person of past acquaintance, there will be no benefit through the instructions when saṃsāra and nirvāṇa separate. Repeated examination and familiarity with the tradition of practice is very important. Thus, be diligent in practice. {124} It is said that "Today, there is no difference between you and Śrī Vajrasattva."

The explanation of the path as the explicit instruction is concluded.

3.1.3 The Mode of Liberation of the Result

There are three topics in the mode of the liberation of the result: (1) the mode of liberation in the natural bardo for those of the highest caliber, (2) the mode of liberation in the bardo of dharmatā for those of the middling caliber, and (3) the mode of liberation in the bardo of existence for those of the average caliber.

3.1.3.1 The Trio of the Highest Caliber

Among the trio of highest caliber, those of the highest of the highest caliber are liberated through the introduction. The *Explanatory Tantra* states:

> Attaining introduction and realization are simultaneous.
> Attaining realization and discarding Dharma are simultaneous.
> Discarding phenomena and the cessation of deluded concepts are simultaneous.
> The cessation of deluded concepts and cleansing of ignorance are simultaneous.
> Cleansing ignorance and expanding pristine consciousness are simultaneous.
> Expanding pristine consciousness and full buddhahood are simultaneous.

Explain the symbolic meaning and be seated in the ranks of
the victors.[185]

Those of the middling of the highest caliber that are liberated through the practice are those who possess the intimate instructions and who are liberated by taking their own place directly as the path. The *Explanatory Tantra* states:

The nāḍī that connects the gem and the ocean
is white, smooth, hollow, and empty,
not tainted with bindu and blood.
Great pristine consciousness arises through it.[186] {125}

Since one practices the meaning of the passage above, the child, self-originated pristine consciousness, arises in the mother, the maṇḍala of dharmatā, self-arising without arising or ceasing. Since one practices self-liberation without joining or parting from it, one is liberated into the three kāyas that are never joined or parted, and the bardo of dharmatā does not appear.

Those of the average of the highest caliber who discard the body are the lazy ones, who are liberated through direct self-recognition of the basis. For example, just as there is no interval between the setting sun and the rising moon on the fifteenth day of the lunar month, [similarly,] there is liberation into plenilunar pellucidity.

While vidyā is unborn and undying, the way the yogi becomes free of the shell of the body is as follows: Since the earth vāyu dissipates into water, the four limbs (*bag bzhi*) fall to the ground, and the body feels heavy. Since the water vāyu dissipates into fire, the mouth and nose become dry. Since the fire vāyu dissipates into air, the heat escapes

185. This citation matches the first two lines of the *Stainless Gem Tantra,* p. 175, line 6. The reader will notice that this passage is identical to the passage in SLB on page 51 in this volume. However, the identity of the text Longchenpa is here calling the *Explanatory Tantra* remains ambiguous because this passage, unlike the previous passage attributed to the *Explanatory Tantra,* does not come from the UT.

186. UT, pp. 445–46. It reads somewhat differently from what is presented here: *// rin chen rgya mtsho sbrel ba ni// dkar 'jam khog pa stong pa'i rtsa// thig le khrag gis ma bkang bar// ye shes chen po kun tu rgyu//.*

from the four extremities of the body. Since the air vāyu dissipates into space, consciousness becomes unclear. At that time, the mind and vāyu leave the lungs, enter into the pathway of the throat, and exit through the doorways of the mouth and nostrils. When [the mind, accompanied by vāyu,] leaves through an exhalation accompanied with the sound *ha*, because these cannot return, this is called "death."

Vāyu and mind are crippled in space. {126} Since there is no vāyu in the lungs, the ambulatory blind horse and the sighted paraplegic are parted, and mind and pristine consciousness are separated. At that time all blood in the body gathers in the life nāḍī. When the blood enters the heart from the life nāḍī, this is called "The king is seated on the throne and the ministers engage in conflict." Though a state of fright and confusion arises, this remains unnoticed by a person's mind. Pristine consciousness leaves the heart center, enters the opening of the pathway—the white silk nāḍī—and when it exits the doorway—the lamp of water—pristine consciousness arises as pellucidity, which is recognized as a self-appearance. Thus, one is liberated into plenilunar pellucidity instantly without the bardo. The *Ornament of Introduction* states:

> At that time, pristine consciousness leaves through the eyes. Since the eyes are focused on the unbroken cord of compassion, there is liberation into plenilunar pellucidity without a bardo.[187]

Further, appearance, realization, liberation, and the emergence of compassion are simultaneous.

3.1.3.2 The Trio of the Middling Caliber

There are three topics for liberation in the bardo of dharmatā for those of middling caliber. Those of the highest of the middling caliber are

187. This is a paraphrase of *Introduction of Buddhahood Tantra*, p. 666, *// de'i dus shes pa rang gi mig la gtad// mig thugs rjes rgyun mi 'chad pa'i thag pa// 'od kha dog lnga la gtad pas// yar gyi zang thal la grol lo//.*

liberated in one instant. In the instant of uprooting saṃsāra, intrinsic radiance manifests as luminosity once the outer and inner objects and mind cease. In the moment of seeing the truth of dharmatā, wisdom that does not grasp to the appearance of the clusters arises. In the vajra-like moment, once one obtains the personal benefit of the dharmakāya, the rūpakāya that is beneficial to others arises. As it is said [in the *Explanatory Tantra*], pristine consciousness arises in the first moment, there is recognition in the second moment, and after being liberated in the third moment, the benefit of others is produced.[188]

Those of the middling of the middling are liberated in six instants. The *Explanatory Tantra* states:

> In the first moment outer and inner delusion cease,
> in the second moment intrinsic radiance manifests as light,
> in the third moment one abides in that light for a moment,
> in the fourth moment wisdom arises within oneself,[189]
> in the fifth moment the fivefold transcendent state is complete,
> and in the sixth moment, there is dissolution into the dharmakāya beyond thought.

Those of the average of the middling are liberated on the fifth day of concentration. The outer elements subside like the sun—the apparent objects of the five senses cease. The inner elements are like dusk—the mind of the group of six ceases. The secret elements are like moonrise—when the appearances of pristine consciousness arise, simultaneously, the cluster of the five families of luminosity also arises, and the stage of certainty is acquired. The *Explanatory Tantra* states:

> The appearances of luminosity arise immediately. {128}
> The wisdom of realization arises gradually.[190]

188. This refers to the passage in UT, p. 455.

189. UT, p. 456, reads *rang snang shes rab* for *rang la shes rab*. PM, p. 270, reads *rang snang skag gcig*.

190. See note 47.

Further, since on the first day one sees blue light and recognizes the empty essence of vidyā as the intrinsic radiance of the dharmadhātu, self-appearances are liberated into the cluster of Vairocana. Since on the second day white light is recognized as the state of the mirror-like pristine consciousness, self-appearances are liberated into the cluster of Vajrasattva. Since on the third day yellow light is recognized as the intrinsic radiance of the pristine consciousness of uniformity, self-appearances are liberated into the cluster of Ratnasambhava. Since on the fourth day red light is recognized as the intrinsic radiance of the pristine consciousness of individual discernment, self-appearances are liberated into the cluster of Amitābha. Since on the fifth day green light is recognized as the intrinsic radiance of the pristine consciousness of successful activity, self-appearances are liberated into the cluster of Amoghasiddhi. The *Golden Rosary* states:

> Abiding in the center and bearing the characteristics
> of white, yellow, red, and green,
> also, each [father] appears in the heart center
> as a group of four:
> a vajra, jewel, lotus, and crossed-vajra.
> Also, the mothers are like the shadow of the body.
> The first maṇḍala cluster
> is a complete form in the seat of the basis.
> Vajrākṣobhya dwells in the middle, {129}
> surrounded by Kṣitigarbha, Lāsya,
> Maitreya, and Dhupe,
> the second maṇḍala cluster.
> Ratnasambhava dwells in the middle,
> surrounded by Akāśagarbha, Māle,
> Samantabhadra, and Puṣpe,
> the third maṇḍala cluster.
> Amitābha dwells in the middle,
> surrounded by Avalokiteśvara, Girti,
> Mañjughoṣa, and Dvipa,
> the fourth maṇḍala cluster.

Amoghasiddhi dwells in the middle,
surrounded by Vajrapāṇi, Nṛti,
Nīvaraṇaviṣkambhī, and Ghande,
the fifth maṇḍala cluster.
Because of manifesting similarly,
they arose from that [maṇḍala cluster]
with form, color, and hand implements resembling those of
the principal.
The six munis engage in the benefit of beings,
the four male door guardians tame them through the four
immeasurables,
and the four female door guardians liberate them from the
four extremes.
Since the dhātu and pristine consciousness are inseparable,
those appear as Samantabhadra and Samantabhadrī.
The mass of concepts is the qualities appearing as the five
kāyas.

At that time, the six higher perceptions arise: The higher perception of the eye sees {130} the buddhafield of the dharmakāya beyond mind above, sees the buddhafield of the saṃbhogakāya in front, and sees the buddhafield of the nirmāṇakāya below. The higher perception of the ear hears the discourse of the speech of the dharmakāya above in one-pointed pristine consciousness, hears the sound of the five pristine consciousnesses of the saṃbhogakāya, and hears the intrinsic sounds of the individual languages of the six realms. The higher perception of mind knows the transcendent state of the dharmakāya above, knows the transcendent state of the saṃbhogakāya in front, and knows the minds of the six classes below. The higher perception of place knows the place of residence of the dharmakāya above, knows the place of residence of the saṃbhogakāya in front, and knows the place of residence of the six classes of nirmāṇakāya below. The higher perception of activity knows all the causes and results of oneself and others. The higher perception of the base of magic powers, through knowing whom to tame with what, emanates the six muni nirmāṇakāyas performing the benefit of sentient beings. Those higher perceptions are called "the nonconceptual eye of Dharma." The mode of those is stated in the *Large Compendium of Tilakas*:

> Nonabiding pristine consciousness is the dharmakāya,
> bearing the characteristics of the five pristine consciousnesses.
> Self-originated pristine consciousness is the five elements,
> arising as the dimension of pure dharmatā.
> The bindus of five colors of light,
> which manifest as five colors—blue, and so on—
> are understood to be the essence of the buddhas of the five families,
> and the five kāyas [are understood to be] the perfect embodiment of pristine consciousness.
> Forty-two [kāyas] manifest as light.
> Each one dwells in the radiance of pristine consciousness,
> which is clear, brilliant, beautiful, and radiates rays of light.
> The celestial mansion of the five pristine consciousnesses
> has the nature of being pervaded with clarity, warmth,[191] coolness,
> vastness, and[192] lightness,
> a blazing mass of pristine consciousness that is the source of all.
> The three seats,[193] which are not generated, are complete in the basis,
> produce emanations through the three unions,
> and remove the darkness of migrating beings' ignorance.[194]

The way the benefit of sentient beings is enacted: Light rays shine

191. Following LCT, p. 208, reading *drod* for *ro*.

192. Following LCT, p. 208, reading *shing* for *zhing*.

193. "Three seats" refers to the five buddha family couples, corresponding to the five aggregates and the five elements; the male and female bodhisattvas, corresponding to the sense organs and sense objects; and the ten wrathful deities, corresponding to the ten joints on the body.

194. LCT, pp. 207–8, line 5. This citation is incorrectly attributed to the *Universal Tilaka*.

from the tongues of the saṃbhogakāya couple, which enter the eyes of a man [and a woman][195] of pure karma and then enter the womb. After [the light rays] transform into a nirmāṇakāya, and after that nirmāṇakāya performs the benefit of taming whomever is to be tamed, it then gathers into the precious secret sheath and abides in the state of a single, great, indivisible interiorized clarity. As such, the uninterrupted benefits performed by emanations are perfect. *Chanting the Names of Mañjuśrī* states:

> Various emanations part into the ten directions,
> performing benefits in conformity with migrating beings.[196]

The way the result is perfect: A perfected one appears as kāyas performing benefits, because vidyā appears as the ceaseless potentiality of compassion. They also are exteriorized clarity that dissolves within, and in the end it is explained that they gather into the state of vidyā. *Chanting the Names of Mañjuśrī* states:

> There is nirvāṇa, nirvāṇa,
> [those] close to excellent nirvāṇa,
> and the one who brings happiness and suffering to an end.
> Liberated and freed, the body of complete liberation
> is not evident, not apparent, does not [need] to be clarified,
> and does not change yet pervades everywhere.

As such, there are five points in the explanation of the inner dhātu of the original purity of liberation: (1) wisdom lifts into space, (2) the elements subside into the mother, (3) pristine consciousness dissolves into the dhātu, (4) wisdom gathers in space, and (5) vidyā takes its own place.

First, the intrinsic vāyu of pristine consciousness generates the rūpakāya within the dimension of dharmatā. The life-sustaining vāyu is purified by these four: Powerful, Keeper of Power, Lifter, and Stabilizer. {133} Powerful inseparably joins together the principal and the retinue

195. This process is described more fully in PM, p. 478.

196. CNMa, 8a.

of the vāyu of pristine consciousness; however, in reality they are inseparable. Keeper of Power instantly generates the five—the principal and the retinue—in the stage of the dharmadhātu. Lifter abides as the rūpakāya in the state of the dharmakāya in which the support and the supported are inseparable. Stabilizer naturally clarifies[197] the nonconceptual transcendent state.

The elements subside into the mother: the five impure elements—the hardness of earth, the moistness of water, the heat of fire, the motility of air, and the pervasiveness of space—are liberated as the five pure elements. Air is well-arrayed as a crossed vajra, the samaya goddess gathers into space, and the unmoving air dissolves into the dhātu. Water is a well-amassed wheel of crystal, and since it gathers into a single dimension, water without moistness dissolves into the dhātu. Since earth is an evenly proportioned stūpa composed of the five kinds of gems in the manner of a tree, earth without hardness dissolves into the dhātu. Fire blazes with light like a lotus, and since it ripens the unripe, fire without heat dissolves into the dhātu. Since space that does not pervade also does not fall, like the tip of a victory banner, space that does not pervade dissolves into the dhātu. {134} The *Universal Tilaka* states:

> As such, since the five elements arose directly from the mother, in the end they are liberated directly into the mother, and because of nonabiding, they subside into the mother.[198]

In the dissolution of pristine consciousness into the dhātu, among the three ways in which the body of appearances dissolves, three appearances dissolve one into the other. The appearance of impure delusion dissolves into the appearance of dharmatā, and the appearance of pure dharmatā dissolves into the appearance of the utterly pure pristine consciousness.

The three eyes dissolve one into the other: The present wisdom eye dissolves into the eye of dharmatā in the bardo, and the eye of dharmatā

197. Reading *mi rtog pa rang gsal* for *mi rtogs pa nang gsal*.

198. UT, p. 473.

dissolves into the eye of pristine consciousness. The eye of wisdom is imperturbable, because it is pure. The eye of dharmatā is fearless, because it is pure. The eye of pristine consciousness is unchanging in the precious sheath—the transcendent state of the interiorized clarity of pristine consciousness—because it is utterly pure.

The three bodies dissolve one into the other: The present body of flesh and blood dissolves into the body of pristine consciousness in the bardo. The body of pristine consciousness dissolves into the body of the secret precious dharmakāya.

There are four topics in wisdom gathering into space: {135} [pristine consciousness is] (1) dissolved but not hazy, (2) clear but not conceptual, (3) existing but selfless, and (4) differentiated but not separated. First, the elements subside into the mother. Pristine consciousness dissolves into the dhātu. Since the three kāyas are inseparable, pristine consciousness abides as interiorized clarity. Second, within the dharmakaya—clear without taints, clear without front or back, clear without above or below, and clear without cardinal or intermediate directions—the kāya of blazing precious light and the kāya of pure self-appearance clearly appear. There is no analytical mind due to the absence of moving vāyu, because there is no body of traces. Third, since the view is self-originated pristine consciousness, it exists but is free from the self of traces. Fourth, the blazing precious five kāyas manifest as individually distinct *mudrās* in a dimension of light within the dimension of the dharmakāya, without opening up the figures with faces and hands or the deluded appearance of the basis, because the inner dhātu is originally pure.

There are four in vidyā taking its own place: (1) There is no change in the dharmakāya, {136} which is a vajra-like kāya. Since the dharmakāya makes vidyā the nature of the rūpakāya, the dharmakāya is imperishable. (2) Since pristine consciousness is unceasing, the nature of longevity, which is like a swastika, is the interiorized clarity of the saṃbhogakāya abiding permanently. (3) The continuous samādhi, which is never joined or parted from, is the transcendent state beyond sessions, like the course of a river. (4) The absence of clarity and obscuration in vidyā, free from all taints like the heart of the sun, is the attainment of intrinsically clear pristine consciousness, abiding without change in the precious sheath. These four are the intimate instruction of being seated on one great throne, the intimate instruction of merging buddhafields into one, the intimate instruction of appearances manifesting in one, and the intimate instruction of gathering into one great sheath. There are no objects for buddhas, no phenomena in pristine consciousness, no self in the result, and no equal[199] in the transcendent state. Even if one could go higher than that, there is no road to go higher.

The great perfected one's sheath of the precious secret has been explained.

3.1.3.3 The Bardo of Existence for Those of Average Caliber

In the bardo of existence for those of average caliber, there is the intimate instruction to avert the extreme of saṃsāra, like repairing an irrigation sluice. {137} The so-called "bardo of existence" occurs after one is free from the body of this life and the appearances of pristine consciousness subside as the self-appearance of the bardo of dharmatā. Since past traces are activated, the body of memory arises like the appearance of a dream, with complete sense organs and in possession of magical powers. One is naturally anxious, unable to remain in one place, going everywhere. One cannot be seen by anyone other those in the bardo or those with the divine eye. One makes effort to find a body and a place to settle. The *Explanatory Tantra* states:

> Since the wisdom of realization did not arise
> in the appearance of the luminosity of the bardo,
> the appearance of past traces is activated.
> One has the form of the body of the previous existence,
> with all sense organs complete and unimpeded.
> One can be seen by those of the same class and those with the
>   divine eye.
> One behaves with the force of the magic power of karma.

199. Reading *mtshung med* for *'tshun med*.

> One searches for a body and a place to settle,
> entering a birthplace by arriving at a deva palace,
> the slopes, a womb, or a cave.
> Hell beings and pretas have mental bodies.[200]

At this time, since one's consciousness is seven times clearer than before, {138} and since the wheel of luminous appearance and the oral instruction of the guru are among the six recollections to be explained, those of the highest of the average caliber avert the extreme of saṃsāra with the thought that it is like an illusion. It is said that they are liberated because they cultivated the generation stage of the pledged deity. Those of the middling of the average think of the qualities of the pure buddhafields and the buddhas, going for refuge to Śrī Vajrasattva in the Abhirati buddhafield in the east, and so on. It is said they are liberated in those buddhafields where they have gone for refuge. Those of the average of the average are elevated by the excellent karma of seeing the key points of the introduction. After they are reborn as a child of faithful parents, due to their positive karma they will meet [with this teaching] in twenty-five or thirty-five years, and they will be liberated without a bardo.

This concludes the extensive explanation of the basis, path, and result.

3.2 The Six Lamps

From among the six topics in the summary points (*gnad bcings*) of the six lamps, the lamp of the abiding basis is the buddhahood of the naturally perfected basis that exists in all saṃsāra and nirvāṇa, just as butter pervades milk. {139} The *Lion's Roar of Śrīmālādevī Sūtra* states:

> The *sugatagarbha* pervades all sentient beings.[201]

Chanting the Names of Mañjuśrī states:

200. This is a rough paraphrase of UT, p. 444.

201. Found in Ratnākaraśānti, *Explanation of the Compendium of Sūtras*, 293b, line 5.

Unchanging, going everywhere, a pervader.[202]

The *Vajrapañjara Tantra* states:

There are no buddhas and no sentient beings
outside of the jewel mind.

The *Preparation of the Four Cakras* states:

The unproduced and nonarisen with a core of five lights
is the supreme basis and foundation of all living beings.[203]

The lamp of the fleshy heart is the kāyas and pristine consciousnesses along with their own light, abiding like a lamp inside a vase. The *Tathāgatagarbha Sūtra* states:

Tathāgatagarbha abides within all sentient beings just as it is originally.[204]

Chanting the Names of Mañjuśrī states:

Personally known without wavering,
the supreme foremost one holds the three kāyas.[205]

The *Hevajra Tantra* states:

Great pristine consciousness abides in the body,
truly free of all concepts,
pervading entities,
abiding in the body, but not arising from the body.[206]

The *Compendium of Tilakas* states: {140}

202. CNMb, p. 339.

203. *'Khor lo bzhi sbags*. Unidentified.

204. Unattested.

205. CNMb, p. 334.

206. *Hevajra Tantra*, 2a–2b.

> The function of the memory of sentient beings is in the center of the heart,
> abiding as an entity of light[207] with three characteristics.[208]

Likened to a white silk thread, the lamp of the smooth white nāḍī is the nāḍī that connects the heart to the eyes, inside of which arises the intrinsic radiance of pristine consciousness, like rays of sunlight through a window. From the *Extensive Sūtra Verses*:

> The pristine consciousness connected with the lamp
> sees all the buddhafields of the ten directions.[209]

Chanting the Names of Mañjuśrī states:

> This explanation of the approach of the illusory net
> is the pure, excellent path.[210]

The *Avataṃsaka Sūtra* states:

> Since the ocean is illuminated from the bottom,
> manifesting in the sky through the path,
> the maṇḍala of light is brilliant.

The *Pellucid Tilaka of Pristine Consciousness* states:

> The king of nāḍīs, the crystal tube,
> exists piercing the sun and the moon.[211]

The lamp of the watery far-reaching laṣso is the pure essence of the eyes, the two doorways of naturally arising pristine consciousness, like the radiance of the sun in the eastern sky shining on a western mountain. The *Mother* states:

207. Following CT, reading *'od* for *nyid*.

208. CT, p. 240.

209. This text is unidentified. The citation in question, however, is found in a text attributed to Vimalamitra: *Explanation of the Path of the Illusory Net*, p. 1028.

210. CNMb, p. 349.

211. *The Pellucid Tilaka of Pristine Consciousness*, p. 165, misidentified as CT.

> The primal nature of the mind is luminosity.[212]

Chanting the Names of Mañjuśrī states: {141}

> The single eye of pristine consciousness is immaculate.
> The tathāgata is endowed with a body of pristine
> consciousness.[213]

The *Greatness of Samantabhadra Existing in Oneself Tantra* states:

> The key point of the direct perception of the self-appearance
> of consciousness
> is the self-appearance of excellent pristine consciousness.[214]

The *Universal Tilaka* states:

> The primordial radiance of clear dharmatā
> is like the morning dawn.[215]

The lamp of the bardo is when one recognizes the appearance of the basis arising as kāyas and pristine consciousnesses, like encountering a person one has previously met. The *Pristine Consciousness at the Time of Death Sūtra* states:

> Meditate on natural, nonreferential luminosity
> without attachment to anything.[216]

Chanting the Names of Mañjuśrī states:

> An illuminating, great light,

212. *Perfection of Wisdom in 25,000 Lines*, vol. *ka*, 123.

213. CNMb, pp. 339–40.

214. This passage reads */shes pa rang snang mngon sum gnad/ legs pa'i ye shes rang snang ba/*. The *Greatness of Samantabhadra Existing in Oneself Tantra* in the BGB, p. 307, reads */rig pa rang gnas mngon sum snang// nyes pa gang gis mi tshugs pa'i// legs pa ye shes rang snang ba'i// mngon par byang chub sku bstan pa'o/*.

215. UT, p. 378, reads */nam langs ba'i nam mkha' lta bu'o/* for */nam langs zhogs pa lta bu'o/*. Longchenpa's reading is the one given here.

216. This passage is a paraphrase of the *Pristine Consciousness at the Time of Death Sūtra*, 153a.

> pristine consciousness is bright as the stars.
> The lamp of pristine consciousness is the lamp of migrating beings,
> a brilliant mass beautiful to behold.[217]

The *Guhyasamāja Tantra* states:

> A great cloud of light rays
> is present in the center of the sky,
> buddhas with blazing light,
> pervading all with blazing pristine consciousness.[218]

The *Compendium of Tilakas* states:

> The multicolored intrinsic radiance arising {142}
> from the great self-originated pristine consciousness
> manifests as the five families.[219]

The lamp of the ultimate result is when the appearance of the basis dissolves into the dhātu and vidyā takes its own place, never moving away from the sheath of the precious secret. There is nothing beyond that and nothing to enhance, like a good harvest in the fall. The *Mother* states:

> Totally beyond the false, the culmination of nirvāṇa.[220]

Chanting the Names of Mañjuśrī states:

> There is nirvāṇa, nirvāṇa,
> [those] close to excellent nirvāṇa.[221]

The *Kernel of All Views Tantra* states:

217. CNMb, p. 334b. In the final line, Longchenpa gives *'lta na sdug* for *'od gsal ba*.

218. This citation is not found in this form in the *Guhyasamāja Tantra*. It seems to be an assembly of several different citations from different Guhyasamāja sources.

219. *Compendium of Outer, Inner, and Secret Most Essential Tilakas*, p. 367.

220. *Heart of the Perfection of Wisdom*, 146b.

221. CNMb, p. 339.

When the Coronation of Pristine Consciousness[222]
is applied to the phenomena of the universe and beings,
saṃsāra and nirvāṇa,
apart from being the kāyas and pristine consciousness,
they do not become saṃsāra's three realms—
everything is the dimension of profound dharmatā.[223]

The *Universal Tilaka* states:

Since the nondual dharmakāya never changes,
the kāya of vajra-like emptiness is attained.[224]

This concludes the summary of the six lamps.

3.3 The Summary of the Key Points of Pristine Consciousness

The summary of the key points of pristine consciousness is that when all the teachings of the bardo are summarized, {143} they are included in the following verse:

The illusory body is cast off.
The movements of one's mind are stopped through vanishing.

222. *Ye shes spyi blugs*, literally "Coronation of Pristine Consciousness," the name of a class of Great Perfection empowerment described in this tantra.

223. *Kernel of All Views of the Great Perfection*, p. 345. The first and last line are unattested in the tantra itself, and Longchenpa gives *spyi blugs* for *chen po*. The entire passage in the tantra itself is */dper na zangs lcags la sogs pa// gser 'gyur rtsi yis btab gyur na// thams cad gser du 'gyur ba las// zangs dang lcags su mi 'gyur bzhin// ma rig rnam rtog msthan ma la// ye shes chen po rgya 'debs na// sku gsum ye shes rang bzhin las// khams gsum 'khor bar mi 'gyur te// gdod nas ma skyes ye sangs rgyas/*: "For example, if copper, gold, and so on, are treated with gold-transformation elixir, all become gold and do not become copper or iron. Similarly, when great pristine consciousness is applied to the characteristics of conceptual ignorance, apart from the nature of the three kāyas and pristine consciousness, they do not become saṃsāra's three realms, having always been buddhahood that does not arise from the start."

224. UT, p. 475.

> The maṇḍala of self-appearance arises instantly.[225]
> Self-originated pristine consciousness is known vividly.
> Original reality is uniformly liberated.

The reasons are:

> Since the illusory body is borrowed, it is discarded.
> Since one's mind is deluded, it ceases.
> Since pristine consciousness has always existed, it arises.
> Since the result is the recognition of one's own state, it is liberation.

When those are summarized, they are included in:

> Self-originated pristine consciousness is known vividly.

Since the self-originated pristine consciousness that abides within oneself is introduced by the guru, understood, and practiced, one is liberated in this life. Since the self-appearance is liberated, one is liberated in the bardo. Since vidyā takes its own place in the sheath of the precious secret, everything is included in self-originated pristine consciousness. As the *Explanatory Tantra* states:

> Everything is the state of self-originated pristine consciousness.[226]

It is said that the basis is primordial buddhahood, the path is evident buddhahood, and the result is perfect buddhahood, {144} steadily merging with the uniform transcendent state of the buddhas.

This concludes the concise topic concerning self-originated pristine consciousness.

225. Reading *tal gyis* for *lta gyis*.

226. This passage does not appear in the UT; however, it does appear twice in Longchenpa's *Collected Miscellaneous Writings of Rgyal-ba Klon-chen rab-'byams-pa*, 2: pp. 421 and 452.

3.4 *Planting the Nail with Five Inscriptions*

Planting the nail with the five inscriptions has five divisions of three: (1) the three times of the arising of the reminder, (2) the three signs of absence of obstacles, (3) the three arguments of not taking birth, (4) the three crucial points of instruction, and (5) the three modes of attaining buddhahood.

(1) The light rays arise as a condition and are recalled. The light rays of the five pristine consciousnesses radiate. The maṇḍala arises as a condition and is recalled. Third, vidyā is pure, and the instructions arise as a condition and are recalled. Perfect buddhahood is the vidyā of the path.

(2) The absence of obstacles regarding symbols is like the water and the moon. The absence of obstacles regarding signs is like a body and its shadow. The absence of obstacles regarding the meaning is the luminosity of dharmatā.

(3) Since the external apprehended objects are pure, there is no place to take birth. Since the inner apprehending mind is pure, there is no self to take birth. Since the maṇḍala of luminosity arises in the sky, birth is cut off.

(4) There is no ground of saṃsāra for saṃsāra; the universe and beings are pure in the basis. {145} There is no ground of delusion for delusion; the universe and beings arise as a maṇḍala. There is no ground of wandering for wandering; the mother and child pristine consciousnesses meet.

(5) From among the three calibers—highest, middling, and average—the highest of the highest caliber attain buddhahood like leaping lions, the middling attain buddhahood in the manner of the union of the sun and the moon, and the average attain buddhahood in the manner of the arrow of a great archer. The highest of the middling attain buddhahood like a hare and snare, the middling attain buddhahood like a *garuḍa* and an egg, and the average attain buddhahood like a small meadow and a herd. The highest of the average attain buddhahood like a traveler arriving home, the middling attain buddhahood like jumping into a

mother's lap, and the average attain buddhahood like a nephew entering the presence of a kind aunt.

That concludes the unmistaken explanation of the key points of the intimate instructions.

3.5 Sealing the Esteemed Teaching

There are three topics in sealing the esteemed teaching.

The seal of the guru: From this time forward, you must not belittle the cause and result of karma. You must not criticize inferior *siddhāntas*. You must supplicate the guru and practice continuously. You must properly guard samaya and keep this secret from others.

The seal of the pledge: Place a statue on the head of the student and say, "Practice the intimate instructions that arise from this and do not explain the secret intimate instructions to those without fortune. If those are explained, a strong punishment will befall you."

The seal of the guardians of the doctrine: "The appointed guardians of this teaching are Śrī Mahākāla, Ekajaṭī, and Vajrasādhu, who are sentinels of the doctrine and will definitely oversee your samaya, evaluating positive and negative. Thus, do not transgress the command and the samayas!"

If the seal of the doctrine is transgressed, one will vomit blood, one's eyes will fall on the ground, and after one dies, one will be born in Vajra Hell. If one violates the entrustment seal, there will be no benefit. If one violates the pledge seal, it will cost one's life. If one trains properly, one will accomplish everything positive in this and future lives and be blessed by all the gurus, pledged deities, and ḍākinīs.

> As such, this essential core of the intimate instructions of the supreme secret
> enables one to cross the ocean of saṃsāra in this life.
> The profound meaning of the definitive, unsurpassed aural lineage
> is a sublime Dharma superior to others, e ma ho! {147}

The meaning of the guru's words, practices, and intimate
instructions,
which were wrapped up and scattered about unclearly,
are here collected in one place, set forth for the benefit of
future generations,
and watched over by the ocean of samaya-bound guardians.

By this virtue, may all migrating beings
obtain the abode of Dharma Lord Guru Samantabhadra,
may the teaching of the aural lineage of luminosity spread,
and may the festival of fortunate, sublime Dharma increase!

The *Ultimate Mirror of the Aural Lineage* was composed on the slopes of Gangri Thökar in the moonlight shining in a grove of a cloud of light rays at Samantabhadra Palace by Natsok Rangdrol, the yogi of the essence of luminosity.

Those with faith in this ultimate Dharma,
with a guru to explain the intimate instructions,
should uphold this until they awaken,
relying diligently on it at all times.

Virtue, virtue, virtue.

The Essential Handbook

Homage to Śrī Samantabhadra.

> I bow to the three kāyas, who radiate one thousand lights of
> naturally perfected activity,
> and to the feet of the lineage gurus of the three lineages. {148}
> I shall write down the most profound intimate instruction,
> the *Essential Handbook,*
> the meaning of the practice of the luminous tilaka.

Here, there are three topics: (1) preparing the basis by ascertaining the key points of the body, (2) finding the path by ascertaining the key points of vāyu, and (3) attaining realization through ascertaining the key points of vidyā.

1. *The Key Points of the Body*

Among these four—the dharmakāya, saṃbhogakāya, nirmāṇakāya, and the posture of inseparability—the lion-like dharmakāya posture is being seated majestically, with the fingers of the hands in a ball, planted on the ground to the right and left of the lungs. The neck is bent at its base, and the eyes are directed into the sky. The elephant-like saṃbhogakāya posture is face-downward, with the knees to the chest. The elbows are planted on the ground, and the palms cover the throat. The *ṛṣi*-like nirmāṇakāya posture is being seated upright while pressing the knees against the chest, with the elbows crossed on the knees. Regarding the vajra-like inseparability posture, it is said:

Vajrāsana is perfect buddhahood.[227]

The feet are crossed, the hands are in equipoise, and the spine and crown are straight like a stack. The neck is slightly curved, and since that corresponds with the spine, the central nāḍī is planted. That automatically stops memory and concepts, {149} and the vāyu is confined as it self-purifies. Train in these four principal key points, which are an important basis of activity for whatever one wants, like one who is cutting a vajra.

2. *The Key Points of the Vāyu*

The path is clarified by ascertaining the key points of the vāyu—expelling, holding, summoning, and retaining. *Expelling* means exhaling slowly as far as the vāyu will go. *Holding* means comfortably holding the exhalation without allowing an inhalation and holding out as long as possible in that state. *Summoning* means inhaling slowly. *Retaining* means maintaining the inhalation as long as one naturally can and putting the vāyu in its place. Since the horse of the mind is vāyu, when the vāyu is held, the mind is held. By holding the vāyu out, the mind is implicitly held inside. This is an amazing key point. One must be careful to only breathe slowly. All purposeful effort will cause obstacles. By allowing the vāyu to move on its own without effort, obstacles will be impossible. In the end, it will seem as if the vāyu does not move at all, and so on.

The qualities arise from understanding the key point of breathing slowly. Beyond that, only vāyu is said to be utmost in importance as the key point of sustaining vidyā, {150} because all increase and exhaustion of the appearances depend on the vāyu. Since the vāyu is controlled in the beginning, the luminosity of appearances increases. Since the vāyu is purified and exhausted in the end, luminosity is free from moving outward, and the inner ground of dissolution is exhausted. Since this key point is extremely important, the knowledgeable must understand

227. CNMb, p. 341.

it. In particular, when strong afflictions arise such as unhappiness or anger, releasing an exhalation with the sound *ha* will cause those to automatically dissipate. When positive feelings such as faith, samādhi, and so on, arise, holding the inhalation will cause those to increase. This is the intimate instruction of this key point.

3. *The Key Points of Vidyā*

From among the three topics of realization through ascertaining the key points of vidyā—the key point of the doorway, the key point of the field, and the key point of vidyā—first is the key point of the doorway, the three gazes. The peaceful śrāvaka gaze is looking downward. The bodhisattva gaze is looking straight ahead. The tathāgata gaze is looking upward. An important point in these gazes is to effortlessly relax the eyes in their natural condition. Overuse of the eyes causes eye strain and tearing, impairs the tissue of the eye, and results in an aversion to gazing. {151} Since one is relaxed in how one gazes, visible appearances increase and the eyes are free of problems.

The key point of the field is to look into the center of the sky free of clouds. The key point of the dhātu is strictly not deviating from a single place. If one sometimes looks here and sometimes looks there, the field of arising for appearances will be absent. Thus look at one place.

The key point of vidyā is to not allow it to slip outside the other sense doorways. Since it is focused without distraction directly on the center of the sky, its radiance is guided outside through the eyes alone. Therefore, whatever momentary memories and concepts arise, those do not exceed the single vastness, and vidyā takes its own place, like a bird flying up to its chicks. From the white light, which is huge and shimmering at first, the five lights and bindus then appear. By focusing the eyes inside of those, outwardly light manifests, inwardly pure radiance is separated, and in between there is uniform nongrasping, all of which come together at the same time. Since outwardly the luminosity of appearance appears as the method, the relative creation stage, and inwardly the luminosity of emptiness arises as wisdom, the ultimate completion stage, vidyā takes its own place in the state of the dharmakāya. {152}

At this time, three things occur: (1) vidyā rests in its own place, like a king who never moves from the throne; (2) since the vāyu subsides, there is no discursive memory or concepts, like ministers held in prison; and (3) as there is no distraction to the other five doorways, luminosity arises in the sky, like the populace arriving to a dance performance. Since the transcendent state is inseparable from the state of dharmatā, vidyā, which is unimpeded in emptiness and clarity, abides in its own place as the naturally perfected three kāyas, and one realizes the essential meaning of the training.

Through that realization, by meditating day and night, since one has no hope or fear with respect to saṃsāra and nirvāṇa, one never moves from the fourth time[228]—dharmatā—and one truly obtains qualities that demonstrate the measure of cultivation, such as predictions by ḍākinīs, and so on.

As such, those of the best cultivation will appear in a sheath of light of pristine consciousness, having purified the sheath of traces and entered the sheath of precious natural perfection in this lifetime. Those of middling cultivation will liberate the sheath of light of pristine consciousness[229] into the sheath of natural perfection through recognition of the luminosity of dharmatā as their own state and vidyā taking its own place. Because those of average cultivation will meet this Dharma in future lives and attain buddhahood, {153} this is the mirror of the secret key point called "the instruction that places buddhahood in one's hand."

> Having gathered the great, secret, definitive key points for
> this approach,

228. A specialized Dzogchen term for going beyond the three times: past, present, and future.

229. *Ye shes 'od kyi sbubs* is another term for the realization of the body of light, *'od kyi lus,* also known as rainbow body, *'ja' lus.* However, those who attain liberation in the bardo "liberate" or discard the sheath of light of pristine consciousness because they attain liberation in a mental body in the bardo of dharmatā.

the yogi who self-liberates diversity[230]
arranged this on the slopes of Gangri Thökar.
By this virtue may all migrating beings attain buddhahood.

This composition by Longchen Rabjam is complete. Virtue, virtue, virtue.

230. A play on *sna tshogs rang grol.*

Abbreviations

BGB: Collection of Tantras of Vairocana
CT: *Compendium of Tilakas Tantra*
CGT: *Blazing Body of the Charnel Ground Tantra*
CNMa: *Chanting the Names of Mañjuśrī, Dg.K*
CNMb: *Chanting the Names of Mañjuśrī, Tsham*
Dg.K: Derge Kenjur
Dg.T: Derge Tenjur
GC: *Great Chronicle*
KST: *Bka' ma shin tu rgyas pa* (Kaḥthog)
LCT: *Large Compendium of Tilakas*
NGB: Collected Tantras of the Ancient
NTY: *Snying thig ya bzhi*
PM: *Zab don gnad kyi me long*
SDP: *Self-Appearing Direct Perception of the Definitive Meaning*
SLB: *Self-Appearing Luminosity of the Bardo*
SAV: *Self-Arising Vidyā Tantra*
Skt: Sanskrit
Tsham: Mtsham brag edition of the *Rnying ma rgyud 'bum*
Toh: A Complete Catalogue of the Tibetan Buddhist Canons
Tib: Tibetan
UM: *Ultimate Mirror of the Aural Lineage*
UT: *Universal Tilaka Tantra*

Bibliography

Canonical Collections

Bai ro'i rgyud 'bum. TBRC W21519. 8 vols. Leh: S.W. Tashigangpa, 1971.

Bstan 'gyur (*sde dge*). Delhi: Delhi Karmapae Choedhey, Gyalwae Sungrab Partun Khang, 1982–85.

Rnying ma rgyud 'bum: a collection of treasured tantras translated during the period of the first propagation of Buddhism in Tibet. Thimphu, 1973.

Rnying ma'i rgyud bcu bdun: collected Nyingmapa tantras of the Man ngag sde class of the A ti yo ga (Rdzogs chen). Prepared from the A 'dzoms lcog sgar blockprints. New Delhi: Sanje Dorje, 1973.

Rnying ma'i rgyud bcu bdun: Rdzogs pa chen po Rnying rgyud nang gsal sems klong sde gsum gyi phyi ma shin tu zab pa man ngag rgyud kyi rgyal po: the Seventeen Tantras of the Rnying-ma-pa tradition that are the sources for the practice of the Rdzogs-chen belonging to the Man ngag class. Thimphu: Druk Sherig Press, 1985.

The Mtshams-brag manuscript of the Rnying ma rgyud 'bum. Thimphu: National Library, Royal Government of Bhutan, 1982.

Kangyur Titles

Buddhāvataṃsaka Sūtra (*Buddhāvataṃsakanāmamahāvaipūlyasūtra*). Dg.K, phal chen, *ka, kha, ga, a* (Toh 44).

Chanting the Names of Mañjuśrī (*Mañjuśrījñānasattvasyaparamārthanāmasaṃgīti, 'jam dpal ye shes sems dpa'i don dam pa'i mtshan yang dag par brjod pa*). Dg.K, rgyud, *ka* (Toh 360).

Collected Verses on the Noble Perfection of Wisdom (*Āryaprajñāpāramitāsañcayagāthā, 'Phags pa shes rab kyi pha rol tu phyin pa sdud pa tshigs su bcad pa*). Dg.K, shes rab sna tshogs, *ka* (Toh 13).

Guhyagarbha Tantra (*Śrīguhyagarbhatattvaviniścaya, Dpal gsang ba'i snying po de kho na nyid rnam par nges pa*). Dg.K, rnying rgyud, *kha* (Toh 832).

Hevajra Tantra (*Hevajratantrarājanāma, Kye'i rdo rje zhes bya ba rgyud kyi rgyal po*). Dg.K, rgyud, *nga* (Toh 417, 418).

Heart of the Perfection of Wisdom (*Bhagavatīprajñāpāramitāhṛdaya, Bcom ldan 'das ma shes rab kyi pha rol tu phyin pa'i snying po*). Dg.K, shes rab sna tshogs, *ka* (Toh 21).

Lion's Roar of Śrīmālādevī Sūtra (*Āryaśrīmālādevīsiṃhanādanāmamahāyānasūtra, 'Phags pa lha mo dpal phreng gi seng ge'i sgra zhes bya ba theg pa chen po'i mdo*). Dg.K, dkon brtsegs, *cha* (Toh 92).

Perfection of Wisdom in 25,000 Lines (*Pañcaviṃśatisāhasrikāprajñāpāramitā, Shes rab kyi pha rol tu phyin pa stong phrag nyi shu lnga pa*). Dg.K, kyi khri, *ka–ga*. (Toh 9).

Pristine Consciousness at the Time of Death Sūtra (*Āryātajñānanāmamahāyānasūtra, 'Phags pa 'da' ka ye shes zhes bya ba theg pa chen po'i mdo*). Dg.K, mdo sde, *tha* (Toh 122).

Samādhirāja Sūtra (*Āryasarvadharmasvabhāvasamatāvipañcitasamādhirājanāmamahāyānasūtra, 'Phags pa chos thams cad kyi rang bzhin mnyam pa nyid rnam par spros pa ting nge 'dzin gyi rgyal po zhes bya ba theg pa chen po'i mdo*). Dg.K, *da* (Toh 127).

Sūtra of the Knowledge that Includes Everything (*Sarvatathāgatacittajñānaguhyārthagarbhavyūhavajratantrasiddhiyogāgamasamājasarvavidyāsūtramahāyānābhisamayadharmaparyāyavivyūhanāmasūtra, De bzhin gshegs pa thams cad kyi thugs gsang ba'i ye shes don gyi snying po rdo rje bkod pa'i rgyud rnal 'byor grub pa'i lung kun 'dus rig pa'i mdo theg pa chen po mngon par rtogs pa chos kyi rnam grangs rnam par bkod pa zhes bya ba'i mdo*). Dg.K, snying rgyud, *ka* (Toh 829).

Tathāgatagarbha Sūtra (*Āryatathāgatagarbhanāmamahāyānasūtra,* 'Phags *pa de bzhin gshegs pa'i snying po zhes bya ba theg pa chen po'i mdo*). Dg.K, mdo sde, *za* (Toh 258).

Vajrapañjara Tantra (*Āryaḍākinīvajrapañjaramahātantrarājakalpa, 'Phags pa mkha' 'gro ma rdo rje gur zhes bya ba'i rgyud kyi rgyal po chen po'i brtag pa*). Dg.K, rgyud, *nga* (Toh 419).

Collected Tantras of the Ancients

Blazing Body of the Charnel Ground Tantra (*Dur khrod phung po 'bar ba man ngag gi rgyud*). In Tsham, 7: 816–39.

Blazing Precious Gem Tantra (*Nor bu rin po che 'bar ba'i rgyud*). BGB, vol. 6: 176–83.

Compendium of Tilakas Tantra (*Thig le 'dus pa'i rgyud*). Tsham, 9: 236–47.

Chanting the Names of Mañjuśrī (*Āryamañjuśrīnāmasaṃgīti, 'Phags pa 'jam dpal gyi mtshan yang dag par brjod pa*). Tsham, 21: 326–49.

Divine Heap of Jewels Tantra (*Lha rgyud rin po che spungs*), BGB, vol. *ca*: 459–501.

Epitome of Secrets Tantra (*Gsang ba yang khol gyi rgyud*). Tsham, 13: 617–21.

Compendium of Outer, Inner, and Secret Most Essential Tilakas (*Phyi nang gsang ba gsum gyi yang zhun thig le 'dus pa*). BGB, 6: 372–83.

Greatness of Samantabhadra Existing in Oneself Tantra (*Lta ba thams cad kyi rgyal po kun tu bzang po'i che ba la rang gnas pa*). BGB, 8: 30–37; Tsham, 4: 187–245.

Guhyasamāja Tantra. Tsham, 18: 752–969.

Introduction of Buddhahood Tantra (*Sangs rgyas ngo sprod pa'i rgyud*). Tsham, 13: 659–67.

Kernel of All Views of the Great Perfection (*Rdzogs pa chen po lta ba thams cad kyis snying po'i rgyud*). BGB, 8: 338–65.

Large Compendium of Tilakas Tantra (*Thig le kun 'dus chen po'i rgyud*). Tsham, 9: 194–236.

Meaning of the Essential Secret of the Wheel of Pristine Consciousness Tantra (*Ye shes 'khor lo gsang ba'i snying po don gyi rgyud*). Tsham, 9: 21–39.

Pellucid Tilaka of Pristine Consciousness (*Ye shes thig le zang thal gyi rgyud*). BGB 6: 306–31; Tsham, 9: 154–79.

Realms and Transformation of Sound Tantra (*Rin po che 'byung bar byed pa sgra thal gyur chen po'i rgyud*). Tsham, 12: 1–172; Adzom 1: 1–205.

Stainless Gem Tantra (*Nor bu dri med rgyud*). BGB, 6: 172–77.

Universal Tilaka Tantra (*Thig le kun gsal chen po'i rgyud*). Tsham, 13: 296–492.

Uprooting Saṃsāra Tantra (*Rgyud thams cad kyi snying po 'khor ba dong dkrug gi rgyud*). In BGB, 6: 14–31; *Rdo rje srin po rno ba rdo rje mchu can gyi rgyud ces bya ba rgyud thams cad kyi snying po 'khor ba dong sprugs chen po'i rgyud/*. Tsham, 21: 697–715.

Tengyur

Anonymous. *Sgra sbyor bam po gnyis pa*. Dg.T, sna tshogs, *co* (Toh 4347).

Candrakīrti. *Introduction to the Middle Way* (*Madhyamakāvatāra*). Dg.T, dbu ma, *'a* (Toh 3862).

Garab Dorjé. *Illuminating the Meaning of the Mañjuśrīnāmasaṃgīti* (*Āryamañjuśrīnāmasaṃgītyarthālokakaranāma, Phags pa 'jam dpal gyi mtshan yang dag par brjod pa'i don gsal bar byed pa zhes bya ba*). Dg.T. rgyud, *tshi* (Toh 2093).

Jñānagarbha. *Verses on Distinguishing the Two Truths* (*Bden pa gnyis rnam par 'byed pa'i tshig le'u byas pa*). Dg.T, dbu ma, *sa* (Toh 3881).

Mañjuśrīkīrti. *Ornament of the Heart.* (*Śrīsarvaguhyavidhigarbhālaṃkāra, Dpal gsang ba thams cad kyi spyi'i cho ga'i snying po rgyan zhes bya ba*). Dg.T, rgyud, *zi* (Toh 2490).

Ratnākaraśānti. *Explanation of the Compendium of Sūtras* (*Sūtrasamuccayabhāṣyaratnālokālaṃkāra, Mdo kun las bdus pa'i bshad pa rin po che snang ba'i rgyan*). Dg.T, dbu ma, *ki* (Toh 3935).

Saraha. *Song of the Treasury of Couplets* (*Dohakoṣagīti, Do ha mdzod kyi glu*). Dg.T, rgyud, *wi* (Toh 2224).

Śrī Siṃha. *Unwritten Aural Lineage of Cutting Saṃsāra from the Root* (*'Khor ba rtsad nas gcod pa snyan rgyud yi ge med pa'i man ngag*"). In BGB, 2: 84; Bstan 'gyur (snar thang), 87: 17–18.

Vasubandhu. *Treasury of Abhidharma* (*Abhidharmakośakārikā, Chos mngon pa'i mdzod kyi tshig le'ur byas pa*). Dg.T, mgon pa, *ku* (Toh 4089).

———. *Explanation of the Treasury of Abhidharma* (*Abhidharmakośabhāṣya, Chos mngon pa'i mdzod kyi bshad pa*). Dg.T, mngon pa, *ku* (Toh 4090).

Vimalamitra. *Lamp That Illuminates the Name and Meaning* (*Nāmasaṃgītivṛttināmārthaprakāśakaraṇadīpanāma, Mtshan yang dag par brjod pa'i 'grel pa mtshan don gsal bar byed pa'i sgron ma zhes bya ba*). Dg.T, rgyud, *tshi* (Toh 2092).

———. *Explanation of the Path of the Illusory Net* (*Sgyu 'phrul dra ba'i lam bshad pa*). In Bstan 'gyur (Snar thang), 77: 1019–33.

Tibetan Collections

Bka' ma shin tu rgyas pa. Chengdu: Ka' thog Mkhan po 'Jam dbyangs, 1999.

Nsga 'gyur bka' ma shin tu rgyas pa. Chengdu: Si khron dpe skrun tshogs pa si khron mi rigs dpe skrun khang, 2009.

Tibetan Works

Anonymous. *Intimate Instruction of the Secret Cycle* (*Gsang skor gyi man ngag*). Tsham, 9: 289–302.

———. *Child of the Compendium of Tilakas* (*Thig le 'dus pa'i bu*). Tsham, 9: 292–95, BGB, 5: 450–52.

Chodrak Zangpo (*Chos grags bzang po*). *Meaningful to Behold: The Hagiography of Drimé Özer* (*Dri med 'od zer gyi rnam thar mthong ba don ldan*). NTY, 6: 511–602.

Chokyi Drakpa (*Chos kyi grags pa*). *Opening the Eyes of the Fortunate* (*Snyan rgyud rdo rje zam pa'i khrid yig skal bzang mig 'byed*). In *Gdams ngag mdzod*, TBRC W20877, 1: 423–46. Paro: Lama Ngodrup and Sherab Drimey, 1979–81.

Chojey Pal, Lhatse (*Chos rje dpal, lhas btsas*). *Collection of Refutations of False Mantra* (*Sngags log sun 'byin gyi skor*). Thimphu: Kunsang Tobgyel and Mani Dorji, 1979.

Dorjé Pal (*Rdo rje dpal*). *Empowerment Rite of the Mind Series* (*Sems sde'i dbang chog bla ma'i zhal gdams*). In *Gdams ngag mdzod*, 1: 197–254. Paro: Lama Ngodrup and Sherab Drimey, 1979–81.

Drimé Özer (*Dri med 'od zer*) (Longchenpa). *Arrangement of Sections* (*Man ngag dum dum khrigs dum bu bdun cu rtsa bzhi pa*). NTY, 5: 19–434.

———. *Collected Miscellaneous Writings of Rgyal-ba Klon-chen rab-'byams-pa* (*Gsung thor bu*). 2 vols. Paro, Bhutan: Lama Ngodrup and Sherab Drimey, 1982.

———. *Conch Writing* (*Dung yig can rgyud kyi khong don bsdus pa sgron ma snang byed*). NTY, 4: 271–430.

———. *Excellent Chariot* (*Rdzogs pa chen po sgyu ma ngal gso'i 'grel pa shing rta bzang po.*") In *Rdzogs pa chen po ngal gso skor gsum dang rang grol skor gsum bcas pod gsum*, 2: 597–765. 1999.

———. *Four-Section Heart Essence* (*Snying thig ya bzhi*). 13 vols. Delhi: Sherab Gyaltsen Lama, 1975.

———. *Great Guide for the Path of the Supreme Secret* (*Yi ge med pa snyan brgyud mchog tu gsang ba lam khrid chen mo*). NTY, 13: 51–55.

———. *Lamp that Summarizes Vidyā* (*Rig pa bsdus pa'i sgron ma*). NTY, 4: 223–36.

———. *Mind Mirror of the Aural Lineage* (*Snyan brgyud thugs kyi me long*). NTY, 13: 67–84.

———. *Mirror of Key Points of the Profound Meaning* (*Snyan brgyud kyi rgyab chos chen mo zab don gnad kyi me long*). NTY, 13: 157–498.

———. *Resting in Primordial Liberation* (*Ye grol sor bzhag*). NTY, 13: 55–67.

———. *Self-Appearing Direct Perception of the Definitive Meaning: The Great Aural Lineage* (*Snyan brgyud chen mo nges don mngon sum rang snang*). NTY, 2: 379–426.

———. *Self-Appearing Pristine Consciousness: The Short Aural Lineage* (*Snyan brgyud chung ngu ye shes rang snang*). NTY, 2: 355–61.

———. *Self-Appearing Luminosity of the Bardo: The Middle-Length Aural Lineage* (*Snyan brgyud 'bring po bar do 'od gsal rang snang*). NTY, 2: 369–79.

———. *Seven Treasuries* (*Mdzod bdun*). 7 vols. Chengdu: Bum skyabs, 1999.

———. *Stainless Space* (*Khregs chod kyi rgyab yig nam mkha' dri med*). NTY, 1: 394–427.

———. *Three Last Testaments of the Buddhas* (*Sangs rgyas kyi 'das rjes gsum*). NTY, 3: 297–314.

———. *Treasury of the Great Vehicle* (*Theg pa'i mchog rin po che mdzod*). *Seven Treasuries*, vols. 5–6.

———. *Treasury of Siddhānta* (*Sgrub mtha' rin po che mdzod*). *Seven Treasuries*, vol. 2.

———. *Ultimate Mirror of the Aural Lineage* (*Snyan brgyud don gyi me long*). In NTY, 13: 84–153.

———. *White Lotus* (*Theg pa chen po man ngag gi bstan bcos yid bzhin nor bu'i mdzod kyi 'grel pa pad ma dkar po*). *Seven Treasuries*, vol. 7.

Gökyi Demtrucan (*Rgod kyi ldem 'phru can*). *Ggongs pa zang thal*. 5 vols. Simla: Thub bstan rdo rje brag e wam lcog sgar, 2000.

Gyara Longchenpa (*Rgya ra klong chen pa*). *Sunlight That Clarifies the Muni's Doctrine* (*Chos 'byung rin po che'i gter mdzod thub bstan pa gsal bar byed pa'i nyi 'od*). In *Bka' ma shin tu rgyas pa* (*Ka' thog*), 43: 7–842.

Khachö Wangpo (*Mkha' spyod dbang po*). *Manual of the Blissful Center of the Sky* (*Snyan brgyud rin po che'i khrid kyi man ngag mkha' dbyings snying po'i bde khrid / (rdzogs pa chen po sems sde a ro lugs)*). In *Gdams ngag mdzod*, 1: 369–84. Paro: Lama Ngodrup and Sherab Drimey, 1979–81.

———. *The Detailed Manual of the Essence of Bodhicitta, the Precious Aural Lineage* (*Snyan brgyud rin po che byang sems snying po'i pra khrid*). In *Manual of the Blissful Center of the Sky*.

Kongtrul, Jamgön. *Catalogue of the Treasury of Precious Instructions* (*Sgrub brgyud shing rta chen po brgyad kyi smin grol snying po phyogs gcig bsdus pa gdams ngag rin po che'i mdzod kyi dkar chag bkra shis grags pa'i rgya mtsho*). In Gdams ngag mdzod, 18: 384–551. Paro: Lama Ngodrup and Sherab Drimey, 1979–81.

Kunzang Dorjé (*Kun bzang rdo rje*). *The Long Explanation of the Vajra Bridge*. In *Klong sde rdo rje zam pa*. In *Bka' ma shin tu rgyas pa* (*Ka' thog*), 31: 22–339, 32.

Lödro Gyaltsen (*Blo gros rgyal mtshan*). *Manual of the Great Perfection Mind Series* (*Rdzogs chen sems sde'i khrid yig*). In *Gdams ngag mdzod*, 1: 281–306. Paro: Lama Ngodrup and Sherab Drimey, 1979–81.

Namkha Dorjé (*Nam mkha' rdo rje*). *Detailed Manual of the Mind Series* (*Slob dpon dga' rab rdo rje nas brgyud pa'i rdzogs pa chen po sems sde'i pra khrid kyi man ngag*). In *Gdams ngag mdzod*, 1: 317–67. Paro: Lama Ngodrup and Sherab Drimey, 1979–81.

Ngwang Palzang (*Ngag dbang dpal bzang*). *Command Sealed* (*Bka' rgya ma*). In *Gsung 'bum, Ngag dbang Dpal bzang*, TBRC W22946, 9: Chengdu, 1999.

Nyima Bum (*Nyi ma 'bum*). *Eleven Topics of the Great Perfection* (*Rdzogs pa chen po tshig don bcu gcig pa*). Lhasa: Bod ljongs mi dmangs dpe skrun khang, 2008.

Orgyen Jigmé Chökyi Wangpo (*O rgyan 'jigs med chos kyi dbang po*). *Clear Explanation of Reality* (*Theg mchog a ti'i man ngag gnas lugs gsal ston*). In Gsung 'bum, *O rgyan 'jigs med chos kyi dbang po*, 4: 673–700. Gangtok: Sonam Topgay Kazi, 1970–71.

Rongzom Chökyi Zangpo (*Rong zom chos kyi bzang po*). *Introduction to Mahāyāna Systems* (*Theg pa chen po'i tshul la 'jug pa zhes bya ba'i bstan bcos*). In *Rong zom bka' 'bum*, 1: 49–343. Thimphu: Kunsang Topgay, 1976.

Tonpa Shenrab (*Ston pa shen rab mi wo che*) and Tapihritsa. *Oral Lineage of Zhangzhung* (*Zhang zhung snyan rgyud kyi gsung pod*). Dégé Par ma. 1 vol. Lhundrub Teng: Dégé Par khang, n.d.

Tashi Dorjé (*Bkra zhis rdo rje*). *Great Chronicle* (*Rdzogs pa chen po snying tig gi lo rgyus chen mo: man ngag brgya bcu dgu'i nang tshan dgu bcu pa*). In NTY, 6: 435–614.

Sengé Wangchuk (*Seng ge dbang phyug*). *Intimate Instruction of Samantabhadra Merging the Three Kāyas* (*Kun tu bzang po'i sku gsum bsre ba'i man ngag*). Tsham, 9: 29–95; BGB, 5: 450–52.

Vairocana. *The Vajra Bridge Aural Lineage* (*Sgrub sde bcu gsum gyi snying po snyan rgyud rdo rje zam pa'i rtsa ba'i gzhung chung*). In *Klong sde rdo rje zam pa'i gzhung pod stod cha*. In *Bka' ma shin tu rgyas pa* (*Ka' thog*), 31: 20–22.

Vimalamitra. *Precious Lamp* (*Rtsa rgyud sgra thal 'gyur gyi 'grel pa rin po che snang byed sgron ma*). Edited by Chogyal Namkhai Norbu. Australia, 2009; *Pan chen dri med bshes gnyen gyi dgongs nyams sgron ma snang byed 'bar ba'i gsang rgyud* (*Sgra thal 'gyur rtsa rgyud 'grel*). Edited by Tsering Gyatsho (*Tshe ring rgya mtsho*). In *Snga 'gyur bka' ma shin tu rgyas pa*, vols. 107–08. Chengdu: Si khron dpe skrun tshogs pa si khron mi rigs dpe skrun khang, 2009.

Zhikpo Dütsi (*Zhig po bdud rtsi*). *Aural Lineage of Aro Yeshé Jungney* (*A ro ye shes 'byung gnas kyi snyan brgyud sprul sku zhig po'i gsung sgros rta ston jo ye'i yig cha rta rin chen dpal gyi phyug dpe las bshus pa'i dpe dkon chos tshan so brgyad*). In *Bka' ma shin tu rgyas pa* (*Ka' thog*), 107: 7–26.

Reference Works

Achard, Jean Luc. *The Six Lamps: Secret Dzogchen Instructions of the Bön Tradition*. Somerville, MA: Wisdom Publications, 2017.

Esler, Dylan. *The Lamp for the Eye of Contemplation*. Oxford: Oxford University Press, 2023.

Higgins, David. *The Philosophical Foundations of Classical Rdzogs Chen in Tibet*. Vienna: Arbeitskreis für Tibetische und Buddhistische Studien, Universität Wien, 2013.

Longchenpa. *Finding Rest in Illusion*. Boulder: Shambhala Publications, 2018.

Mathes, Klaus-Dieter. *Maitrīpa: India's Yogi of Nondual Bliss*. Boulder: Shambhala Publications, 2021.

Norbu, Namkhai. *Drung, De'u and Bön: Narrations, Symbolic Languages and the Bön Tradition in Ancient Tibet*. Dharamshala: Library of Tibetan Works and Archives, 1997.

———. *Light of Kailash: A History of Zhang Zhung and Tibet*. 3 vols. Arcidosso: Shang Shung Publications, 2009–15.

Norbu, Namkhai, and Adriano Clemente. *The Supreme Source*. Translated by Andy Lukianowicz. Ithaca, NY: Snow Lion Publications, 1999.

Palmo, Ani Jinba. *The Great Image: The Life Story of Vairochana the Translator*. Boulder: Shambhala Publications, 2004.

Smith, Malcolm. *The Blazing Lamp Tantra and the Threaded String of Pearls*. Somerville, MA: Wisdom Publications, 2020.

———. *Buddhahood in This Life*. Somerville, MA: Wisdom Publications, 2016.

———. *The Self-Arisen Vidyā Tantra: A Translation of the Rigpa Rangshar*. Somerville, MA: Wisdom Publications, 2018.

Sparham, Gareth. *Abhisamayālaṃkāra with Vṛtti and Ālokā*. 4 vols. Fremont: Jain Publishing, 2012.

Vasubandhu. *Abhidharmakośabhāṣyam.* Translated by Louis de La Vallée Poussin. English translation by Leo M. Pruden. Berkeley: Asian Humanities Press, 1988–90.

Index

E

K

L

About the Translator

Born in 1962, Malcolm Smith was raised in Western Massachusetts. Captivated by the sound of Tibetan ritual music in 1984, he began his study of the Dharma. He met his first formal teacher, H. H. Sakya Trizin, in 1989. He studied Buddhist philosophy and Tibetan language under the guidance of Khenpo Migmar Tseten for the next five years at Sakya Institute for Buddhist Studies in Cambridge, Massachusetts. In 1990 Malcolm travelled to Nepal to receive Lamdré from the late H. H. Sakya Dagchen.

Malcolm received his first Dzogchen teachings from Chögyal Namkhai Norbu in 1992. In 1993 he met his second Dzogchen teacher, Khenpo Jigme Phuntsok, receiving important transmissions. During this year he entered a three-year solitary retreat. In 1998 he met H. H. Penor Rinpoche and received the complete empowerments of the mahāyoga section of the Nyingma Kama as well as teachings on the Namchö preliminary practices. In 2001, Malcolm met his third Dzogchen teacher, the late Kunzang Dechen Lingpa, from whom he received the *Nyinthig Yazhi* in its entirety, as well as the formal Ngakpa empowerment in 2004. He met his fourth Dzogchen teacher, H. H. Taklung Tsetrul Rinpoche, in 2001, from whom he received the entire transmission of the Gongpa Zangthal in 2010, as well other transmissions. He received the transmission of the Seventeen Tantras from Khenpo Tenzin Thinley in 2012 and again from Tulku Dakpa Rinpoche in 2022. Since 2018, he has been studying under Khenchen Namdrol Tsering of

Namdrol Ling Monastery. In addition, Malcolm has received Sakya, Kagyü, and Nyingma teaching cycles from many other lamas.

Malcolm Smith was awarded the title of ācārya by Khenpo Migmar Tseten of Sakya Institute in 2004. In 2008 Malcolm was granted the title of lama by Lama Ngawang Tsultrim, abbot of Dhongag Tharling. In 2009 Malcolm graduated from Shang Shung Institute of America as a doctor of Tibetan medicine, completing an internship in Xining, in the Amdo province of northeast Tibet.

Since 1992 Malcolm Smith has worked on a wide variety of texts for Sakya, Drikung Kagyü, and Nyingma groups, as well as medical and astrological texts.

What to Read Next from Wisdom Publications

Buddhahood in This Life
The Great Commentary by Vimalamitra
Translated by Ācārya Malcolm Smith
Foreword by Chökyi Nyima Rinpoche

"I rejoice and praise Ācārya Malcolm Smith's direct translation from Tibetan into English of the *Aural Lineage of Vimalamitra.* Since it is certainly of great benefit to those faithful practitioners of Dharma around the world, I sincerely wish that once they have realized the secret of the mind in dependence on all of the book's instruction, which appear through the intimate instructions of the guru, they will be able to accomplish liberation into the body of light in one lifetime."
—Tulku Dakpa Rinpoche

Dzokchen
A Commentary on Dudjom Rinpoché's "Illumination of Primordial Wisdom"
B. Alan Wallace

"Düdjom Rinpoché was a great master and scholar of Dzokchen, and for many years represented the Nyingma lineage-in-exile. This book is a treasury of profound advice and instruction on Dzokchen practice, and would be of immense benefit to all those seeking guidance on this path."
—Jetsunma Tenzin Palmo

Meditation for Modern Madness

His Eminence the Seventh Dzogchen Rinpoche

"This book by His Eminence Dzogchen Rinpoche is offered in the manner of a gift for the entire Dzogchen lineage and is a must-read for Buddhists in general and for Buddhist scholars whose motivation, minds, and goals are vast."—from the foreword by His Eminence Alak Zenkar Rinpoche

The Self-Arisen Vidya Tantra and The Self-Liberated Vidya Tantra

A Translation of the Rigpa Rang Shar and

A Translation of the Rigpa Rangdrol

Malcolm Smith

"Malcolm Smith's translation of these two tantras has opened a door to fundamental, previously inaccessible Nyingma teachings. With a comprehensive knowledge and experience of the subject, Smith has created an erudite translation that is not only accurate but also clear in meaning and beautiful to read. This work is an important milestone in the translation of Tibetan Buddhist texts."—Peter Alan Roberts, translator of *The Mind of Mahāmudrā*

The Tantra Without Syllables and The Blazing Lamp Tantra

A Translation of the Yigé Mepai Gyü and Its Commentary and

A Translation of the Drönma Barwai Gyü and Its Commentary

Malcolm Smith

"The Seventeen Tantras of the Quintessential Secret Heart Essence cycle of the Great Perfection have the potential to reveal directly the genuine realization of clear light. They are the source of all Heart Essence teachings. . . . The blessings of this lineage are forever present and fresh in the sacred words of these sources. In fact, they are the origin from which all information about this pinnacle cycle of the Great Perfection is derived."—from the foreword by Lama Chönam and Sangye Khandro

About Wisdom Publications

Wisdom Publications is the leading publisher of classic and contemporary Buddhist books and practical works on mindfulness. To learn more about us or to explore our other books, please visit our website at wisdom.org or contact us at the address below.

Wisdom Publications
132 Perry Street
New York, NY 10014 USA

We are a 501(c)(3) organization, and donations in support of our mission are tax deductible.

Wisdom Publications is affiliated with the Foundation for the Preservation of the Mahayana Tradition (FPMT).